# Explore ARIZONA!

## by Rick Harris

*Maps by the author*

*Golden West Publishers*

# Dedication

This book is dedicated to those who have pursued the elusive road along with me, including all members of the Friedonian Society for the Preservation of Fun, plus the following: Adam Fried, Mark Fried, Danny Scott, Jeff Kingston, Steve Lamaide, Bonnie Sanders and Jeff Pfunder.

It is the above mentioned who have unselfishly provided this writer with the necessary vehicles of access to the sites described herein.

**Library of Congress Cataloging-in-Publication Data**

```
Harris, Richard L.
   Explore Arizona!

   Includes index.
   1. Arizona--Description and travel--
Guide-books. 2. Historic sites--Arizona--Guide-books.
3. Natural history--Arizona--Guide-books. I. Title.
F809.3.H37  1986        917.91'0453        86-14306
ISBN 0-914846-24-8 (pbk.)
```

**Golden West Publishers**
4113 North Longview Ave.
Phoenix, AZ 85014, USA

Cover design by **Bruce Robert Fischer**

Printed in the United States of America

# Contents

Introduction . . . 4

Cathedral Caves . . . 6

Little Colorado . . . 8

Strawberry Crater . . . 10

Kingston Ruins . . . 12

Old Cliffs Road . . . 14

Mormon Lake Arrowheads...16

Boynton Canyon . . . 18

Loy Butte Drive . . . 20

Beaver Creek Ruin . . . 22

Montezuma Lake . . . 24

The Other Castle . . . 26

Adama's Cave . . . 28

Cornville Ruins . . . 30

Lava River Cave . . . 32

Wingfield One & Two . . . 34

Dewey Ruin . . . 36

Lynx Creek Ruin . . . 38

Senator and Venzia . . . 40

Swansea . . . 42

Crystal Hill . . . 44

Quartz Tour . . . 46

Vulture Mine . . . 48

Copperopolis . . . 50

Indian Mesa . . . 52

Pfunder Ruin . . . 54

The Flumes . . . 56

Nipper Ruin . . . 58

Castle Cleo Ruin . . . 60

Seven Springs . . . 62

Mount St. Claire . . . 64

Papago Clay Pits . . . 66

Petroglyph Canyon . . . 68

Pueblo Grande Canals . . . 70

Lamaide Field . . . 72

Gila Bend Ruin . . . 74

Haufer Wash Ruin . . . 76

Huens Ruin . . . 78

Mustang Ruin . . . 80

Potato Hill Ruin . . . 82

Fossil Creek . . . 84

Verde Hot Springs . . . 86

Peralta Massacre Site . . . 88

Fish Creek Tour . . . 90

Miami Artifacts . . . 92

Cherry Creek . . . 94

Reymert . . . 96

Copper Hill . . . 98

Kinishba Ruin . . . 100

Arsenic Cave . . . 102

Eagle Creek . . . 104

Pima Butte Pottery . . . 106

Gila Butte Pottery . . . 108

Marks Artifacts Spread . . . 110

Chuichu Caves One . . . 112

Chuichu Caves Two . . . 114

Ventana Cave . . . 116

Tumamoc Hill . . . 118

San Agustin Mission . . . 120

Peppersauce Cave . . . 122

Forts of Sonoita . . . 124

Index . . . 126

Explore Arizona Map . . .
                    inside back cover

# Explore Arizona!

Every year, thousands of tourists stream through Arizona without fully appreciating the beauty that surrounds them. Yet, their numbers are small compared to the vast numbers of Arizonans who rarely leave the city to explore the great expanse of outdoors in our state.

Few know where to go other than our fine national parks and monuments. Still, after you have seen Montezuma's Castle, Sunset Crater and Tuzigoot several times, why go again?

We all want to experience some new place, a place where few people go, away from the souvenir shops and mass-produced trinkets—just away from it all!

It is the intention of this book, *Explore Arizona*, to guide you and your lust for adventure into areas of our state that meet these demands, while at the same time, requiring nothing of you except some simple respect for a very fragile environment.

If you are one of those people, restless in spirit, the maps herein will lead your spirit deep into the heart of Arizona. Now, with book in hand, on any weekend, you will find yourself traveling through tortuous, twisting canyons, entwined with the motherly hug of a wide cavern laced with stalagmites and stalactites, or strolling beside a silver stream, hidden by sprawling groves of pine, sycamore or aspen. The choice is yours!

And, on the following weekend, take a short jaunt down the highway and off to the right—to a cliff dwelling, river and dell—the perfect spot for a picnic. Stay for a night or for several days, but don't stay too long or you may stay for a lifetime! Our Arizona can be addicting to the senses!

*Explore Arizona* will help you overcome the guess work—which road to take? what's over there? what will we find when we get there?

If you want to find out, go and look, but rest assured that many things await you over the hill, around the bend and through the thicket. The hiker will want to climb, the hunter will be looking for game. The photographer seeks a perfect vista to shoot from, while the naturalist simply wants to look. The archeologist will find many sites to study remains of people long gone, and the rockhound will have his chance to study coveted crystals and gems. The lucky ones will find remains or traces of creatures or plants that inhabited the earth long before man ever saw the light of day.

As for the rest of us, we only ask for a place where we can stop dodging cars and phone calls, a place to go when we have been fired and feel as though we've just been hired. We want to get the feeling of God, or

Nirvana, or something we cannot quite identify, but we know it's out there, somewhere. And, it *is* out there, clear through Arizona. Each location in this book is selected for a variety of reasons, suitable for a variety of people.

Now, I'm making big claims, so you might be a little leery of the validity of the information contained herein. First, let me tell you that I have been to each site at least three times in a lifetime (hey, I'm just a young tad) of searching the backroads. As a native-born Arizonan, it has been my pleasure to meet an assortment of folks who hold one thing in common, an extreme love for Arizona. Not counting the sites that I found from sheer curiosity, many have been shown to me by other native Arizonans. At times, directions were scrawled on a matchbook cover, or on a ketchup-stained napkin, and others were related orally by the explorers who had been there earlier. I've been rewarded and I've been disappointed, but only the rewards are included in this book, sites for which I possess a certain feeling that can hardly be put into words. As for the maps, they are designed so that you can find the rewards as I did, but minus the hassle of the ketchup-stained napkin.

As for your expectations, well, don't get your hopes up too high. You won't find any outhouses except on the highway. There are no diners and few gas stations. Sometimes you'll find pavement, but mostly not. If you're a can collector, I'm sorry. If you like to collect bumper stickers and porcelain plates, again, I'm sorry.

About all you're going to find at any of these sites is a stray deer or two, some chipmunks, an old fort ruin, an old Spanish mission in ruins, a lot of Indian ruins, and just a lot of outdoor stuff without the frills of modern society. But, hey, isn't that what you're after?

I used to think the days were gone when people lived and died in their towns without seeing the other side of the mountain, but this must still be so, for I know of those who have yet to see beyond the smog-shrouded buildings in front of them. Be you from a small town or a large city, this book has been put together so that you might find another world. Arizona is a place not only to live in, but to breathe in and revel in, and to be enraptured with for all your days. It takes but a little time, a little gas, and a little map to find treasures which are in every stream, every mountain, every cavern, every canyon, and every forest of Arizona.

Gather your friends together, take your family, or just roam by yourself if you wish, and set off to explore Arizona!

Rick Harris

# 1.  *Cathedral Caves*

These caverns are a "must" for the spelunker or even the adventurous at heart.

Once a favored haunt along Route 66, these caverns are now forgotten to most of our state's travelers. As you will find, there has been vandalism dating back to the early twenties, yet the major formations remain intact and are well worth a visit.

Plan on spending an entire day here.

## SPECIAL NOTES:

As in all caves, care should be taken to protect the head from low-lying ceilings.

Also, never travel in caverns without a flashlight. (Flares and candles will *not* do and the former can be especially dangerous because of the fumes.)

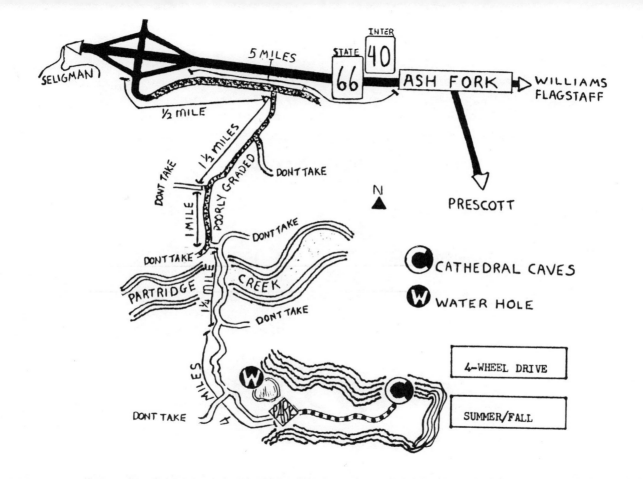

# 2. Little Colorado

This trip is designed for the photographer who would like to have that "new" angle from which to shoot the scenic Little Colorado River.

Taking the main Wupatki road, you come to what is known as the Lomaki ruin, and here a very rough road branches off towards the river.

There are also a number of rarely-visited ruins in the general area where you will be parking that make excellent pictures.

## SPECIAL NOTES:

At the Lomaki turnoff, there is a sign that asks the visitor not to enter this road, and you should request permission at the main museum from one of the rangers on hand. Simply tell the ranger of your intentions.

Also, the Crack in the Rock ruin is located on Monument property, and nothing can be legally gathered from this spot.

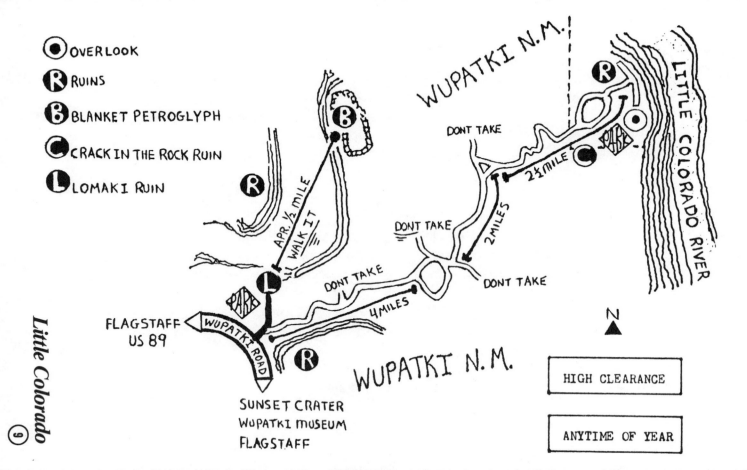

Little Colorado

9

# 3. *Strawberry Crater*

If you have decided against the Little Colorado tour, you may want to consider an alternate trip to Strawberry Crater.

This one spot offers a unique vista from which to photograph the surrealistic terrain of this region, along with a total of seven different Indian ruins that abound in arrowhead material.

Five of the ruins are on top of and around the rim of the crater.

Spend an afternoon, but come prepared to climb.

## SPECIAL NOTES:

The collection of pottery shards in this state is prohibited by law, and this law includes even the tiniest piece you might find.

Also, something unrelated, I recommend that you have a good set of tires on your vehicle and an inflated spare. The ground here is blanketed by finely-crushed lava rock that can wreak havoc on a bald tire.

**S** SUNSET CRATER
**B** BLACK MOUNTAIN
**R** RUINS
**I** ICE CAVES

R R

LAVA BED
(ABOUT 1¾ MILES LONG)

WUPATKI

DONT TAKE

¼ MILE

½ MILE

DONT TAKE

ABOUT 2¾ MILES

US 89
FLAGSTAFF
(visitor Center)

BOUNDARY

**B**

FS 546

DONT TAKE

**I**

MONUMENT

**S**

2¾ MILES

POWER LINES

WUPATKI

N

HIGH CLEARANCE

SPRING/FALL

*Strawberry Crater*

⑪

# 4. *Kingston Ruins*

Here we come upon a neat little package of ruins abandoned by the ancient Anasazi Indians during their migrations to the high mesas that are familiar to us all.

Even though they have been pot-hunted hundreds of times, there still remains an excess of materials that can give you some idea of how they once lived.

Spend the morning here. Don't forget your camera! This way, you will take only memories of this part of Arizona and its vanished culture, and leave the material evidence for future generations to examine.

**SPECIAL NOTES:**

The road will creep up on you, and due to conditions since the last time I was there, it might not even look like a road anymore.

Also, these ruins are not on the reservation, but, out of respect to the Hopi Indians and to the law, pick up nothing, leaving the rooms as you found them.

R RUINS

SUNRISE

RUINS

POWER LINES

ALMOST 2 MILES

IR 15

N ▲

CINDER CONES

FLAGSTAFF

5½ MILES

1¾ MILE

DON'T TAKE

DON'T TAKE

1 MILE

½ M

R

R

R

R

R

SAN FRANCISCO WASH

WINONA

FLAGSTAFF

180 US

WINSLOW

HIGH CLEARANCE

SPRING/FALL

*Kingston Ruins*

⑬

# 5. Old Cliffs Road

Some people have a certain uneasy feeling when it comes to exploring areas that are adjacent to a National Monument, yet, often they find that the most scenic parts can be found outside the fence.

This is my conclusion on Walnut Canyon. Either of the roads indicated on the map will take you to within yards of the canyon rim, and to an overlook that few ever experience.

If you are "into" trees and canyons, this area is a scene of Olympian beauty.

## SPECIAL NOTES:

Don't try to climb down into the canyon, for there are sheer drops that mean death to the tenderfoot.

Also, you may find, as did we, a number of shallow depressions along the rim, and around your camp.

These are the only remains of prehistoric pit houses, and one can find arrowheads in and around the locale. Nevertheless, pottery must be left where you find it.

FLAGSTAFF

I17 — SEDONA CAMP VERDE PHOENIX

US 180 — WINSLOW

N

ANY CAR

2½ MILES

OLD CLIFFS ROAD

180

MONUMENT BOUNDARY

⅛

**R** RUINS (PIT HOUSES)

**F** FLAGSTAFF COCONINO C.C.

**G** GRAVEYARD

**C** CLIFF DWELLINGS

**W** WALNUT CANYON NATIONAL MONUMENT

ANY TIME

PARK

PARK

WALNUT CANYON

# 6. *Mormon Lake Arrowheads*

Not even fishermen know of this spot, but it is well known to people who live in the surrounding area.

On top of the plateau to your right (if you are coming in from Clints Well), there are two very large areas that are literally covered in arrowheads after a heavy summer rain storm.

Please leave these items for others to experience.

**SPECIAL NOTES:**

When examining arrowheads, you should be careful not to cut your fingers on edges that are sometimes razor sharp.

The arrowheads around here are of that nature.

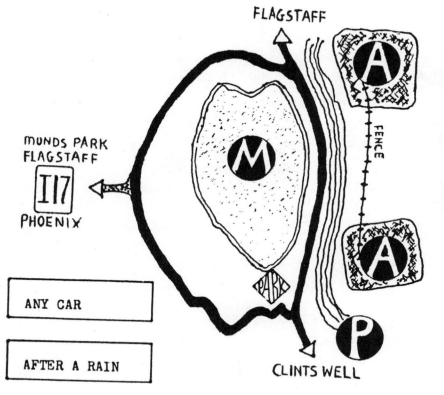

FLAGSTAFF

MUNDS PARK
FLAGSTAFF

I17

PHOENIX

FENCE

CLINTS WELL

ANY CAR

AFTER A RAIN

**M** MORMON LAKE

**A** ARROWHEADS

**P** PLATEAU

N

*Mormon Lake Arrowheads*

# 7. *Boynton Canyon*

The cliff dwellings of Boynton Canyon are the ones that no one wants to tell you about, and are the same ones you always knew to exist.

Local residents do not like to give away their secrets, and it took me quite a few beers to pry this information from an innkeeper.

Now, some of the caves are inaccessible, and others are worth the climb. Yet, if common sense and a fear of heights stop you, they can still be reached by camera.

## SPECIAL NOTES:

Again, you are going to come upon a situation where pretty pieces of prehistoric pottery will tempt your stubborn will.

And, again, the law is even more stubborn legislating against this weakness. Take nothing!

CLIFF DWELLINGS

OAK CREEK C.C

BOYNTON CANYON

BAD ROAD

SEE MAP #8

ABOUT 1½ MILES

LONG CANYON ROAD

VULTEE ARCH

N

2 MILES

DRY CREEK RD.

SHADOWS DR.

SOLDIER PASS

FLAGSTAFF

89A

SEDONA

179

I 17

HIGH CLEARANCE

SPRING/SUMMER

*Boynton Canyon*

⑲

# 8. Loy Butte Drive

Loy Butte contains another cliff dwelling that was related to me by the innkeeper, but what he failed to warn me about was the road.

Now, word has it that this same road, which we found to be anything but a road, has been fixed since our last journey there in mid-1982, but adventurers should plan on finding a wagon trail.

You can make it in by hiking along this "trail," and you can take some good pictures, too—ones that will rival anything you may have seen in *Arizona Highways*.

Plan on spending a day.

**SPECIAL NOTES:**

You are going to be around some ranches that might invite the curious, but you might invite some rock salt on private land.

Respect the "No Trespassing" signs, and respect your feet, too. Wear hiking boots.

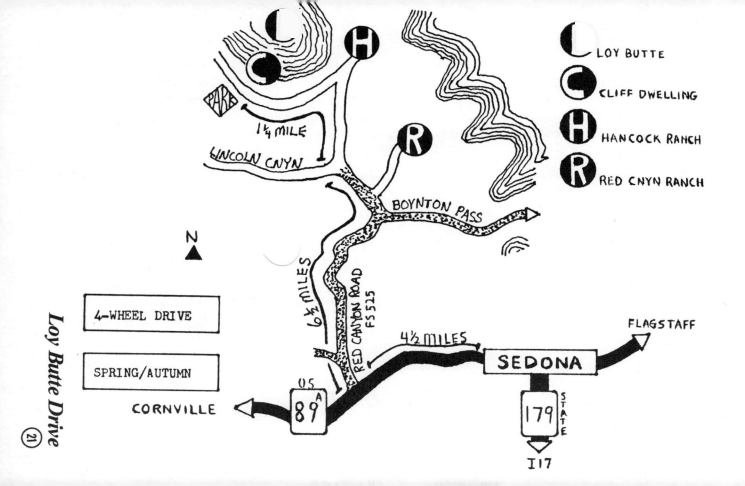

LOY BUTTE

CLIFF DWELLING

HANCOCK RANCH

RED CNYN RANCH

PARK

1¼ MILE

LINCOLN CNYN

BOYNTON PASS

N

4-WHEEL DRIVE

SPRING/AUTUMN

6½ MILES

RED CANYON ROAD FS 525

4½ MILES

FLAGSTAFF

SEDONA

CORNVILLE

US 89ᴬ

179 STATE

I 17

*Loy Butte Drive*

㉑

# 9. Beaver Creek Ruin

At the same watering hole, I chanced to meet a ranger who asked me if I had ever been atop Sacred Mountain along Beaver Creek.

You see, this particular ruin is blanketed with a large variety of artifacts. You name it, it's up there!

And now, much to his relief, I might add that we respected the laws which prohibit the removal of artifacts, but we did come away with some beautiful memories.

### SPECIAL NOTES:

Chances are that you are going to find pieces of pottery that beg a position on your livingroom coffee table. However, there is a "catch" here.

If you are found with that half-bowl in your possession, the rangers from the nearby station will slap you with a fine that could pay for a thousand salad bowls.

Just a friendly warning from your friendly author.

I17 → FLAGSTAFF

SEDONA ← STATE 179

2¼ MILES

CAMP GROUNDS

M F

PHOENIX ← I17

M MONTEZUMA'S WELL

F FOREST SERVICE

R RUINS

ANY CAR

N

ANY TIME

BEAVER CREEK

3/4

MESAS

R SACRED MOUNT.

CAMP VERDE

*Beaver Creek Ruin*

㉓

# 10. *Montezuma Lake*

I spent a great deal of my younger years living at Montezuma's Lake during the summertime, and it was at this very ruin that I first experienced the joys that are found among the ruins.

I have fond memories of this hilltop fortress, and would really like to see it left as is. For this reason, I debated whether or not to include it with my maps.

All I can ask is for you to have respect for this ruin, taking nothing more than pictures.

**SPECIAL NOTES:**

While you are in this area, you might want to stop in at the clubhouse and have a beer. I'm a bar fanatic and a connoisseur of heavy potables who has drunk with the worst of them.

Here, you can drink with the best, savoring hospitality at its best. Everything is the best up here. Beware of angry geese.

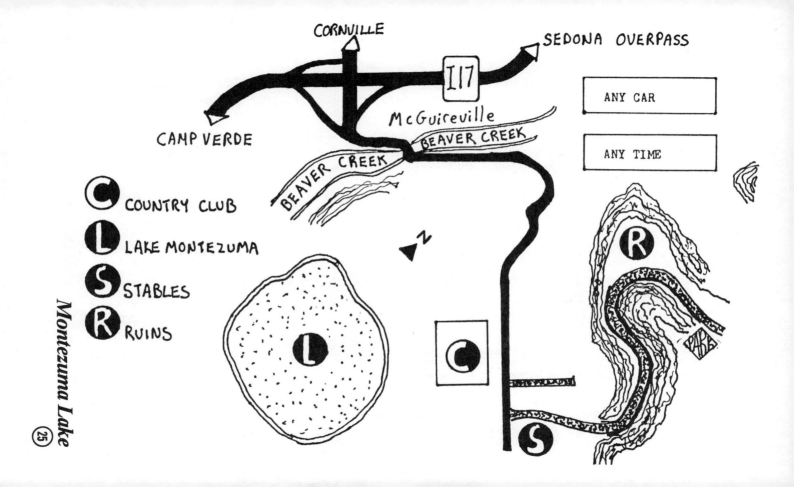

CORNVILLE

SEDONA OVERPASS

I17

ANY CAR

ANY TIME

CAMP VERDE

McGuireville

BEAVER CREEK

BEAVER CREEK

BEAVER CREEK

**C** COUNTRY CLUB

**L** LAKE MONTEZUMA

**S** STABLES

**R** RUINS

L

C

R

S

# 11. *The Other Castle*

An experience at Montezuma's Castle prompted me into writing this book. If you have been to Montezuma's Castle before, you may know that you can no longer enter any of the ruins along the trail. That makes the place downright boring these days.

Now, if you want to change that, these cliff dwellings are for you, and they offer—from the final cave—an excellent vantage point from which to photograph the castle. You'll have a picture that you have never seen in a magazine!

**SPECIAL NOTES:**

There is a drawback to all this, and that is the *dangerous* foot path in front of the dwellings. It is extremely narrow, and the rock is very crumbly. In fact, a friend of mine almost went off the side the last time we were up there.

*Use caution, and if it looks too dangerous for you, go back!*

Nothing can be legally gathered from these caves, so, take your photographs and you will have souvenirs and memories of "the other castle."

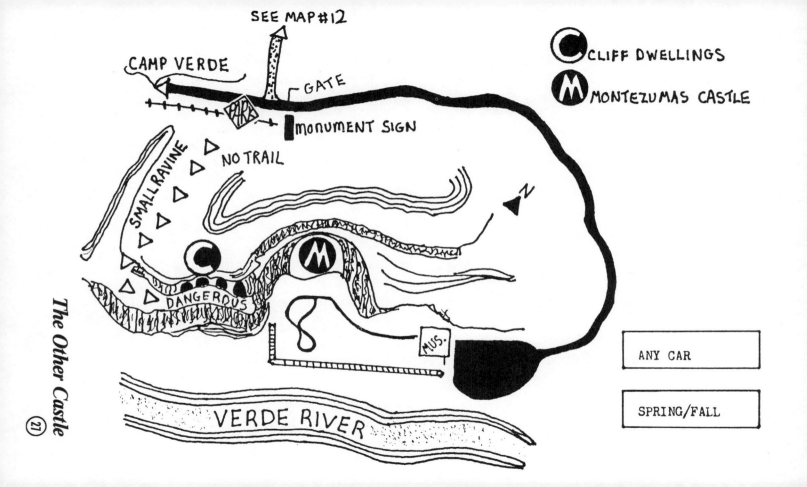

# 12. Adama's Cave

The location of the double caves was first pointed out to me by one Adam "Boogie with Baba" Fried, founder and president of the Friedonian Society of Spelunkers and Muff Divers. It is this same man who kindly leaves a roll of toilet paper in the double caves each year to aid the ill-equipped hiker.

As for Carl's Cave, this where you are heading for, for here is a large cave that has a fantastic accumulation of arrowheads.

**SPECIAL NOTES:**

First, you have to crawl a bit through Carl's Cave, and you will need a good flashlight to do this.

Second, you will notice that the ceiling is cracked, and it could go, but when it will is uncertain. One thing that is certain is that it has gone before.

After going through the second doorway, you will see what I mean, and in the long crack beside the fallen ceiling, you will see arrowheads. Do not remove the artifacts.

first ROAD

I17
CAMP VERDE

MONUMENT SIGN

VARIOUS CABINS

**M** MONTEZUMA'S CASTLE

**D** DOUBLE CAVE

**A** ARTIFACT SPREAD

**C** CARL'S CAVE

N

M

Cross

VERDE RIVER

ADAMA'S

D

A

C

MONUMENT BOUNDARY FENCE

VERDE RIVER

ANY CAR

SPRING/FALL

ODD ROCK SINK

RAVINE

Adama's Cave

29

# 13.  Cornville Ruins

There is a story about how I came upon these ruins, but the memory of a hundred dollar fine—the second one in my illustrious career—makes the story too painful for me to relate. Let me simply state that even the most inconsequential artifact is enough to draw a fine, because it is illegal to remove artifacts from the ruins.

Enough said on that subject. Just check out these ruins and stop off at the confluence of Oak Creek and the Verde. You'll get great pictures here!

**SPECIAL NOTES:**

Before hiking any area of the state, you may want to study topographic maps of the area. These can be found in many hiking or outdoor supply stores and they are available in the public library.

Always be sure to pack along clothing for both hot and cold weather. Desert temperatures can reach 120 or more during the day and fall to 20 at night.

Never leave your vehicle if it breaks down. A stranded vehicle is usually found before the victim, who would not have been a victim had he/she stayed with the car.

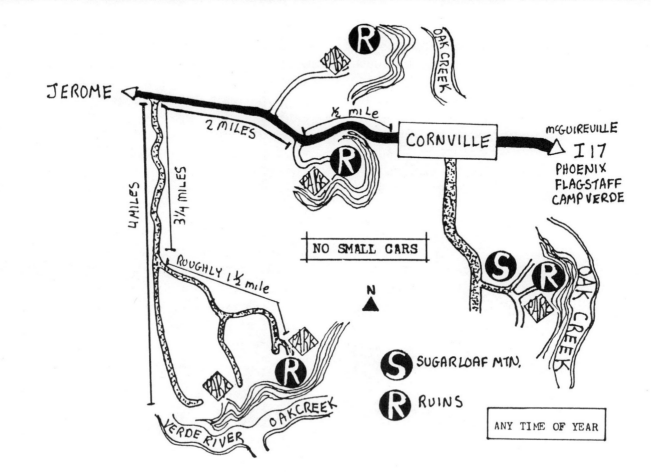

# 14. Lava River Cave

Recently, I found out that the Ice Caves at Sunset Crater have been closed. Therefore, I have omitted a ruin in order to give you the location of another lava tube, one that makes the Ice Caves look sick, as you will learn after wandering a mile or two through Lava River Cave.

When you turn in on Forest Road 171A, you may be wondering where the cave could be, but bear with us. The entrance is obscured by the rock wall in front of you.

Take along a sweater.

## SPECIAL NOTES:

On any trip, take along waterproof matches, a compass, clear plastic, fishing line, hooks and other small survival items. Kits are usually sold at hiking outfitters.

Make sure that your vehicle is in good running order, and use appropriate vehicles for travel conditions that are outlined on each map.

"Any car" means a car supplied with plenty of gas, full of oil, a full radiator, good tires, belts and hoses.

Do not take small economy cars into areas indicated, due to factors that might do injury to the car. High clearance is often indicated, as is four-wheel drive.

¼ M

PS  171A

**L**

N
▲

**L** LAVA TUBE

**W** WILD BILL HILL

**W**

HIGH CLEARANCE

ANY TIME

6½ MILES

FS 171

INT
**40**

BELLEMONT

PARKS

FLAGSTAFF

# 15. Wingfield One and Two

Do you want caves, and cliffs, and cliff dwellings?

Wingfield has it all, or perhaps I should say the Wingfield area. Indeed, if your heart desires an adventure, listen up!

You want to start out at Clear Creek camp grounds, and do so with plans to stay a weekend. If you camp out, you'll have the time it takes to fully explore 97 cliff dwellings, the time to fish the Verde (use corn!), and the time to see a snake or twelve (use feet—run!).

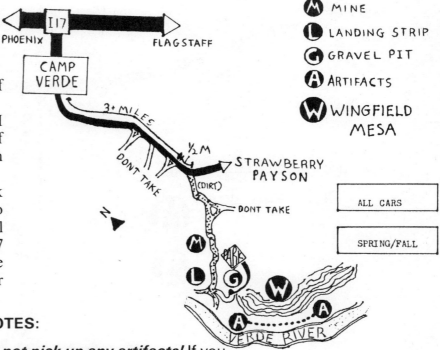

**M** MINE
**L** LANDING STRIP
**G** GRAVEL PIT
**A** ARTIFACTS
**W** WINGFIELD MESA

ALL CARS

SPRING/FALL

## SPECIAL NOTES:

I really cannot stress this enough: ***Do not pick up any artifacts!*** If you are caught with one of those grinding stones or axe-heads like those found in the Wingfield ruins, you may be fined up to $10,000. You can buy a lot of stones or axes for that amount of money!

*Wingfield One*

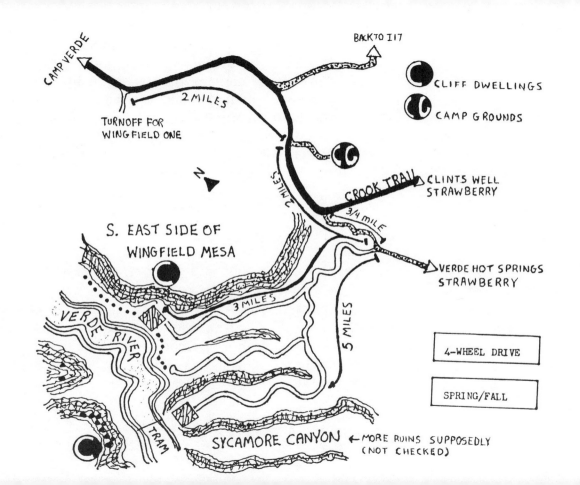

BACK TO I17

CAMP VERDE

TURNOFF FOR
WINGFIELD ONE

2 MILES

CLIFF DWELLINGS

CAMP GROUNDS

N

CROOK TRAIL

CLINTS WELL
STRAWBERRY

2 MILES

3/4 MILE

S. EAST SIDE OF
WINGFIELD MESA

VERDE HOT SPRINGS
STRAWBERRY

VERDE RIVER

PARK

3 MILES

5 MILES

4-WHEEL DRIVE

SPRING/FALL

TRAM

SYCAMORE CANYON

← MORE RUINS SUPPOSEDLY
(NOT CHECKED)

# 16. Dewey Ruin

If you happen to be on your way to Prescott some day, and happen to have an hour or two that can be spared, you might take the time to stop in over at the Dewey Ruin.

Now, when compared to the other ruins listed in **Explore Arizona,** this one is weak when it comes to a concentration of arrowheads.

However, I have been told that there exists a number of prehistoric trash mounds nearby, and if you are luckier than I was, you may just discover them. Good luck!

## SPECIAL NOTES:

When you are in and about ruins, you may find that there is very little to find. Obviously, these ruins have been picked clean by arrowhead hunters and those who illegally pick up pottery shards.

Therefore, you must look away from the ruin in search of those areas where the Indians disposed of their "garbage."

Look down the sides of ravines, in natural gulleys. Follow the course made by runoff from rainstorms.

Picking up artifacts here is also illegal.

PRESCOTT

STATE
69

HIGH CLEARANCE

ANY TIME

2 3/4 MILES

GRAPEVINE GULCH

P

P PUEBLO RUIN

N

2 MILES

TRACKS

DEWEY

STATE
169

CAMP VERDE

CORDES JUNCTION

# 17. Lynx Creek Ruin

"No Trespassing" signs send many a person packing, but not this boy.

Instead of going back, I'm the one who presses forward in search of the person who put up the sign, so as to gain permission of entry. This, rather than going ahead anyway and risk getting a butt full of buckshot.

On a small knoll, across the creek, your ruin lies, but it is also accompanied by a set of said signs. What you want to do is go over to the Victorian mansion and ask someone for permission to photograph the ruin.

### SPECIAL NOTES:

If the man in charge has avoided an argument as to "why" you can't go up there, chances are that he will re-open the door and give you the okay.

Remember to let your head drop when he says no. We have done this three times, and I know of others who have done the same. It worked every time. Know also that you will be watched. So take some pictures, and be sure to dangle the camera from around your neck.

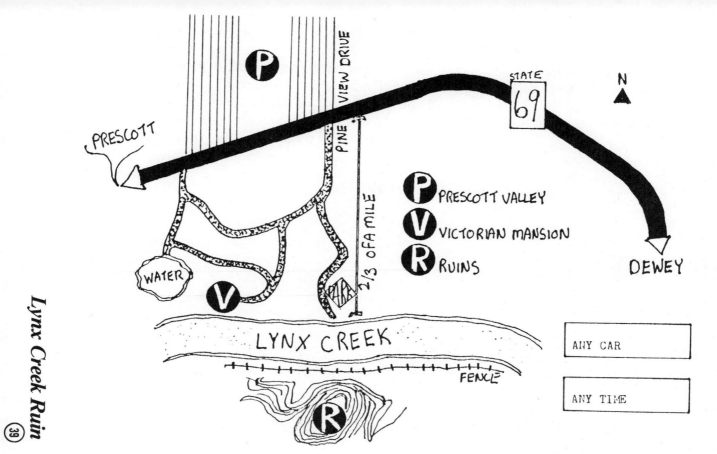

# 18. Senator and Venzia

This book also deals with ghost towns—well-preserved ghost towns that is, or at least towns where you can still spot old bottles, mine equipment, etc.

Now, quickly, the Senator mine might be worth your while, but it has been barred and entry is curtailed.

Secondly, the Monte Cristo mine is intact, and bottles can be found in good condition. However, crazies hang out up there.

And, as for Venzia, don't let the little plaque fool you. Look back in the woods and you will find that tumbled buildings do exist, and still, many a photographic prize.

## SPECIAL NOTES:

Mine shafts can be most dangerous. Don't you remember that "Rifleman" episode when Luke got trapped?

Anyhow, when you enter mine shafts, you do so at your own risk, and it is the same way when you enter into any ghost town.

Banana-brains often live in those places, and their minds are scrambled with "gold fever." If you ever run into one of them, just give the guy a can of beans and haul-ass back to your car.

Also, taking pictures of one of them is like pulling the trigger on his gun.

STATE 69 → PRESCOTT VALLEY

PRESCOTT

US 89 → KIRKLAND JCT.

7¼ MILES

1½

¼ mile

PARK

**S** SENATOR (GHOST TOWN)

**H** HASSAYAMPA LAKE

**V** VENZIA (GHOST TOWN)

**M** MONTE CRISTO MINE (RUINS)

**S** **H** → PRESCOTT

2 MILES

→ SPRUCE MOUNTAIN

4 MILES

PARK

**V** → HORSETHIEF BASIN

HASSAYAMPA RIVER

N

ANY TIME

NO SMALL CARS

*Senator and Venzia*

41

# 19. *Swansea*

You are now looking at a map that will lead you to my favorite ghost town in the whole wide west.

If you're familiar with hunting down supposed ghost towns and have found people still living there, or one solitary building, don't lose hope, because Swansea is very much abandoned and full of buildings.

You can walk down actual streets, poke around in miners' houses and look into a massive mine.

However, you should watch out for snakes. We came upon one angry rattler in one of the houses, but we gave him a can of pork-and-beans and he calmed right down.

**SPECIAL NOTES:**

Seriously, you should be on the watch for snakes.

One of the reasons that mine shafts are so unsafe is the fact that these stupid creatures fall into them all the time. Sure, the rotten timbers and fragile ceilings have something to do with it, but they don't kill as fast as a scared and hungry snake.

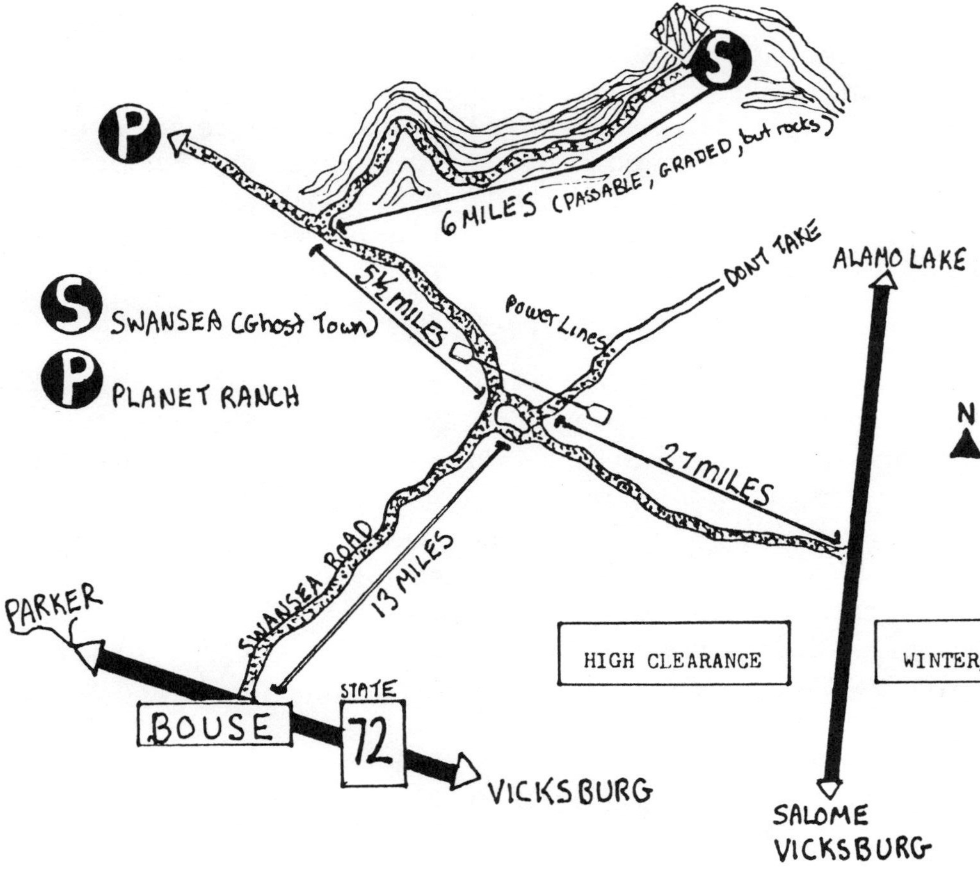

S (circle) — at top right

P (circle) — at upper left

6 MILES (PASSABLE; GRADED, but rocks)

5½ MILES

DON'T TAKE — Power Lines

ALAMO LAKE

**S** SWANSEA (Ghost Town)

**P** PLANET RANCH

N ▲

27 MILES

13 MILES

SWANSEA ROAD

PARKER

BOUSE

STATE 72

VICKSBURG

| HIGH CLEARANCE | WINTER/SPRING |

SALOME VICKSBURG

# 20. Crystal Hill

Have you ever wondered where all those expensive quartz crystals come from?

Well, there is no need to wonder any longer. Pay only for your gas and beer, the crystals you seek are here!

Now you will find some good camping spots at the base of the hill, so sit down for the night. Rise the next morning and spend the day poking around the crevices, and about the top, for these are the spots where you are most likely to discover your better crystals.

And, if you start to feel a little greedy, please, kick yourself in the head, because Mama Nature only pulls this trick once, and others (just like you) would like to see what she has done.

### SPECIAL NOTES:

Don't drink and climb. I almost lost my life for the fifteenth time doing that. Also, believe what the Coors guy is saying: beer does go bad in the heat, just like drunks go mad in the heat.

Seriously, though, if I had any way of proving it to you, I would do so. *When you are hiking, simply do not drink.* I'm sure that many a hiking accident has been the result of some clown getting too drunk to do what really takes all of one's mental ability. I know, for I have been one of those clowns.

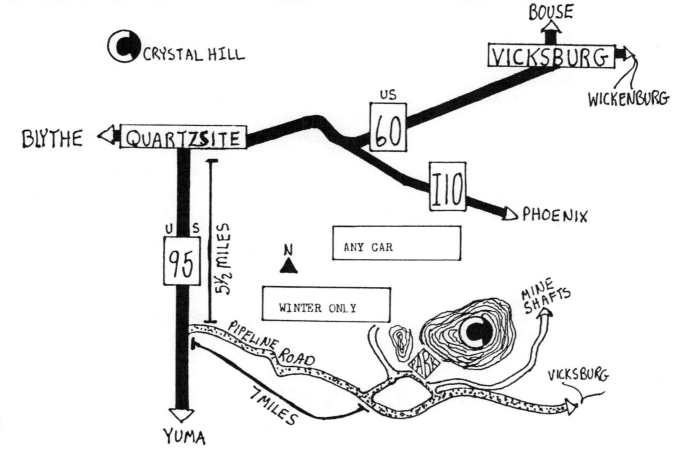

CRYSTAL HILL

BOUSE

VICKSBURG

WICKENBURG

US 60

BLYTHE ◄ QUARTZSITE

I10

PHOENIX

US 95

5½ MILES

ANY CAR

N

WINTER ONLY

PIPELINE ROAD

MINE SHAFTS

7 MILES

VICKSBURG

YUMA

# 21. The Quartz Tour

Date Creek is another spot that abounds in good quartz crystals, and even a few gold nuggets can be found here.

As for Quartz Mountain, well, I've found some of the milky variety around there, but the main attraction is the quartz boulders and larger stones.

**SPECIAL NOTES:**

All roads on the Quartz Tour lead out of Wickenburg, one of my favorite towns in Arizona.

If you're into collecting various specimens of rock, you will find that some of the stores here sell very fine "display" stones, comparable in quality to those that you find at the Mineral Museum in Phoenix.

Also, there are two locations for collecting smoky quartz and amethyst which we have never been able to find. The two roads which *supposedly* lead to these mines are on the old Constellation Road that is reached before entering Wickenburg.

KINGMAN

B BLACK MOUNTAIN

M QUARTZ MOUNTAIN

W WINDMILL

C QUARTZ CRYSTALS

ST. 93

C

C

W

PARK

A

N

DATE CREEK

AROUND 19 MILES

ALAMO LAKE

ALAMO ROAD

WICKENBURG

B

SMALL BLUFF

B

11 MILES

US 60

BLYTHE AGUILA

1¼ mile

DON'T TAKE

DON'T TAKE

M

PARK

HIGH CLEARANCE

WINTER/SPRING

89 U.S.

PHOENIX

# 22. *Vulture Mine*

The only drawback about visiting the Vulture is that you have to pay the owner before you can go snooping around his town.

Also, you're going to find that some guy follows you about the place, staying at a not-so-discreet distance in his truck.

If you are not looking to pick up a bottle or two for nothing, this won't really bother you.

Your time will be spent in wonderment of the beautiful preservation of this ghostly haunt.

**SPECIAL NOTES:**

There is also a cemetery about a mile down the road. You might want to check it out even though little is left.

See, I give you your money's worth, but don't let it go down the drain. If a friend wants to borrow your copy of **Explore Arizona,** tell him to buy his own, because you know he won't return your copy.

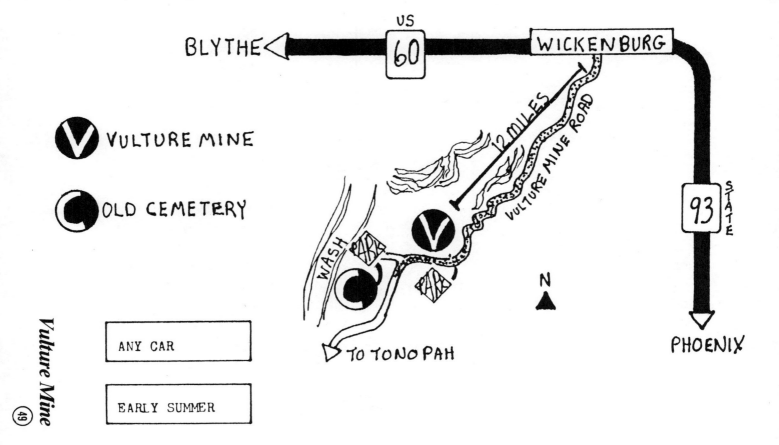

BLYTHE

US 60

WICKENBURG

🅥 VULTURE MINE

🅒 OLD CEMETERY

12 MILES

VULTURE MINE ROAD

WASH

PARK

PARK

N

93 STATE

TO TONOPAH

PHOENIX

ANY CAR

EARLY SUMMER

# 23. *Copperopolis*

I included Copperopolis for several reasons, foremost of which would be the bits and pieces of turquoise that a rock-hound buddy would not admit exist.

I had to set him straight, and shove his nose into them. He made a pendant in the shape of Arizona for my trouble and thirty bucks.

Secondly, I've always enjoyed this ghost town because nobody ever goes up there, until now, that is.

Plan on spending a day, and a couple of bucks on a snake-bite kit.

## SPECIAL NOTES:

Now, I can tell you not to go into mine shafts, and you may or may not heed this advice.

If you do not, at least go into the shaft as prepared as you possibly can. If you don't own a good 500-ft. rope, buy one, and the same goes for a hard hat, high-beam flashlight and good hiking boots.

I even take along an old leather jacket, because of the scrapes and bruises that inevitably result. Besides, the temperature below ground is usually cool.

C COPPEROPOLIS (ghost town)

B Briggs (ruins)

R RANCH

S CASTLE HOT SPRINGS

C

1½ MILES

B

5 MILES

DON'T TAKE

CASTLE CREEK

2¼ MILES

N

WICKENBURG

US 89

R 3 MILES

14 MILES

3 MILES

S

MORRISTOWN

4-WHEEL DRIVE

SPRING/FALL

state 93

PHOENIX

LAKE PLEASANT

*Copperopolis*

51

# 24. *Indian Mesa*

Indian Mesa is a site that is well known to those hunters who straggle up this way in search of the fearsome, the dangerous, the fire-breathing javelina.

I came in search of a ruin that is really magnificent. This because the walls are basically intact. Sure, this ruin has had its fair share of the pothunter's spade, but that which they have left behind makes this climb a worthwhile one. You are likely to see arrowheads lying about.

The pottery and manos must not be touched, and you know why.

**SPECIAL NOTES:**

The most dangerous part about coming up to this ruin is that hunters seem to love this area.

You get these guys all hopped up on cheap beer and they'll shoot at anything.

CORDES JCT.

DONT TAKE

AGUA FRIA RIVER

4 MILES

2 MILES

DONT TAKE

NEW RIVER

I 17

3/4 m

W WINDMILL

A ARTIFACT SPREAD

R RUIN

W

A

R

INDIAN MESA

N

HIGH CLEARANCE

SPRING/FALL

PLEASANT ROAD

NEW RIVER

PHOENIX

# 25. *Pfunder Ruin*

This ruin was first brought to my attention by one of those "devil-may-care" types who was willing to risk the life of his Datsun on these "back roads of Morocco."

It is comparable to the ruin atop Indian Mesa, but with a small difference. Apparently, settlers came this way, or perhaps it was a lone gold miner, for you can find the name "Pfunder" scratched into the cliff. This, accompanied by the date of "84" beneath it.

### SPECIAL NOTES:

The hunters that you really want to watch out for are the ones with machine guns.

You see, they think that Adolph Hitler was reincarnated as a javelina, and after they've had a few, you may look like a javelina to them.

Now, unrelated, a lot of people like to leave their names on cliffs and such, but I have a more permanent and personal method of leaving your mark. We take personal cards and records and place them inside beer cans, burying them beneath stones, so as not to disturb the environment.

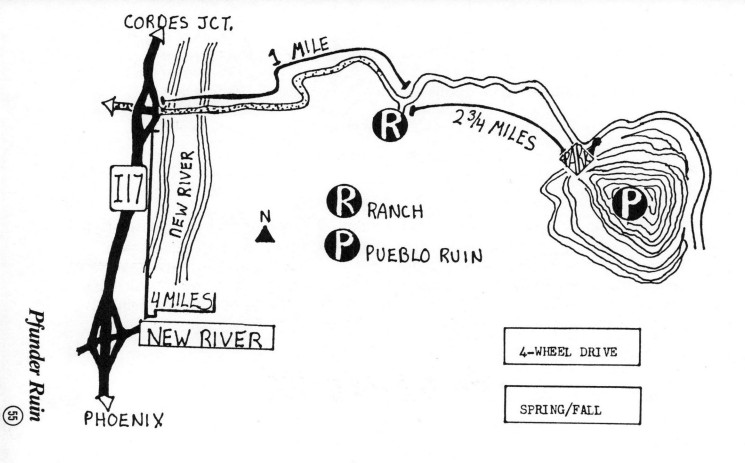

CORDES JCT.

1 MILE

2¾ MILES

I17

NEW RIVER

N

Ⓡ RANCH

Ⓟ PUEBLO RUIN

PARK

P

4 MILES

NEW RIVER

PHOENIX

4-WHEEL DRIVE

SPRING/FALL

# 26. *The Flumes*

In my old high school days, this was the fun place to be on weekends. In fact, as far as we were concerned, this one spot was more popular than the Salt.

Well, the day came when the Sheriff's Department did its number by kicking everyone out after a drowning incident.

In later years, we were told, and came to believe, it had been roofed with concrete slabs. Let me assure you that it has not been covered, and is still a great place to ride your tube or ATC if you choose.

**SPECIAL NOTES:**

If you look closely at the map, you will notice that I have pinpointed a trouble area—the whirlpool.

*It can kill you,* as I can testify to having almost drowned there myself. So, you want to avoid it.

*Do not think you can start at the slide and get out before you reach the whirlpool. You can't!*

**F** FLUMES

DANGEROUS WHIRLPOOL

STRAIGHT AWAY

EASY BEND    FLUME BRIDGE

SLIDE          SLIDE

START
EASY BEND

ENLARGEMENT

LAKE PLEASANT

C.A.P.

FLOW

**F**

FLOW

ANY CAR

¼ MILE

AGUA FRIA

PARK

DROP POINT

1 MILE

BEND IN ROAD

N

LAKE PLEASANT ROAD

SUMMER

SAND

PICK UP ALONG HERE

5+ MILES SUN CITY

# 27. *The Nipper Ruin*

This is an all-around fantastic place to spend a Sunday alone, with friends or family.

Some folks choose to come out and shoot skeet, while others race about on their ATC's. You may enjoy a cave or two and that's what you will find: two caves with little more than a shelter, and the other going in a ways.

Ah, but we must not forget the pueblo ruins and its little spread of arrowheads. All you have to do is keep an eye to the ground in what I have labeled as being an artifact spread.

**SPECIAL NOTES:**

It's been pot hunted clear down to pottery shards, but *even if you find a few, you can't take them.*

Also, there is another ruin on the map which is much smaller in size, and hard to get to because the road has been cut by erosion.

FLUMES

R

LAKE PLEASANT

P

A

C

N

AGUA FRIA

PARK

5 MILES

MAILBOXES

JOMAX ROAD

LAKE PLEASANT ROAD

P PUEBLO RUIN

A ARTIFACT SPREAD

C CAVES

R RUIN

ANY CAR

ALI YEAR

SUNCITY          AND          PHOENIX

10th AVENUE

# 28. Castle Cleo Ruin

This ruin is right in the backyard of Phoenix, and due to its proximity, has also suffered the indignity of shovel rape, so much so that few shards remain in the ruin itself.

But, you are not after the illegal booty of pottery. You want to see arrowheads that can only be found on the eastern slope of the mountain.

Also, note that the ruin is an interesting one in itself, with some walls standing more than five feet.

**SPECIAL NOTES:**

You really don't want to take a car up these slopes unless it is owned by someone you really hate. Then, by all means feel free to have your "friend" take the road and lose his transmission.

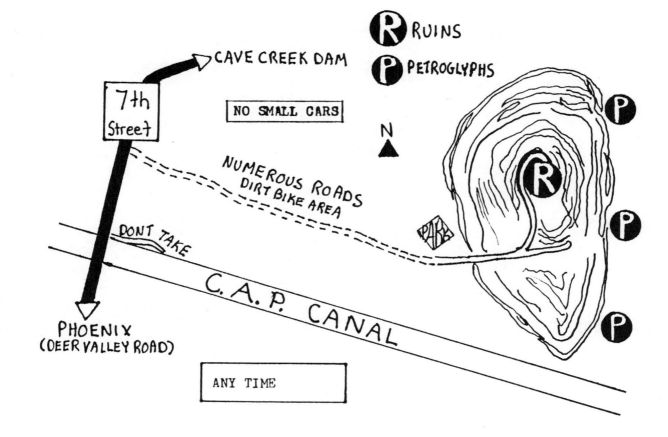

CAVE CREEK DAM

7th Street

**R** RUINS

**P** PETROGLYPHS

NO SMALL CARS

N ▲

NUMEROUS ROADS
DIRT BIKE AREA

DONT TAKE

PARK

C.A.P. CANAL

PHOENIX
(DEER VALLEY ROAD)

ANY TIME

# 29.  Seven Springs

The map says much more than I can in the small space that has been alloted to me.

Nevertheless, let me state that the main attraction is the swimming hole—one that is encompassed by smooth, milky-blue boulders, and fed by a small waterfall that cascades through the rocks, locally known as Nipper Falls.

Swing from the trees, take a sun without benefit of clothing, drink spring-cool water or spring-cooled beer, but pack out your trash.

## SPECIAL NOTES:

You can either park by the ranger station or at the camp grounds if you wish to spend the night.

But, whether you do or not, ***don't camp in between the two!*** You will see signs that warn of this, and if you decide to ignore them, as we did last time, you can expect a visit from some guy who does not hesitate in sticking his shotgun in the direction of your head.

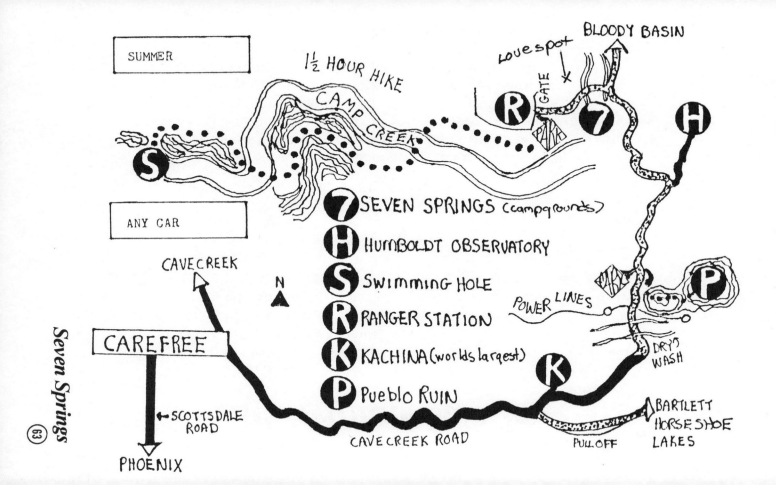

SUMMER

1½ HOUR HIKE

BLOODY BASIN

Love spot

GATE

CAMP CREEK

**R**

**7**

**H**

**S**

ANY CAR

CAVE CREEK

N

**7** SEVEN SPRINGS (campgrounds)

**H** HUMBOLDT OBSERVATORY

**S** SWIMMING HOLE

**R** RANGER STATION

**K** KACHINA (worlds largest)

**P** PUEBLO RUIN

POWER LINES

**P**

CAREFREE

**K**

DRY'S WASH

SCOTTSDALE ROAD

CAVE CREEK ROAD

PULLOFF

BARTLETT HORSE SHOE LAKES

PHOENIX

Seven Springs

⑥③

# 30. *Mount St. Claire*

This ruin equals Tuzigoot in size, and for my money, it is far more interesting.

Now, if you like to climb, you're going to have your bootsfull on Mount St. Claire, for there is no direct path to the ruin. However, we have found it to be easily surmounted with a climb from the rear.

There are plenty of arrowheads to see up there, and for some strange reason, there are more in and about the small ruins by the spring.

**SPECIAL NOTES:**

The Indians have a legend about this ruin that I will relate in part.

It seems that many moons ago a tribe of invisible talking pumpkins inhabited the ruins, but were driven out by root rot to stalk the countryside, never settling down again.

The Indians also say that there are still some of these talking pumpkins living, but that they only appear to drunks and heavy drug users.

7 SPRINGS

**R** RUINS
**S** SPRING
**C** CORRAL

ST. CLAIRE

HORSESHOE LAKE

**R**

**S**

CAVE CREEK ROAD

N

DON'T TAKE

3½ MILES

6½ MILES

BARTLETT DAM ROAD

**C**

CAREFREE

1¼ MILE

NO SMALL CARS

SPRING/FALL

BARTLETT LAKE

# *31. Papago Clay Pits*

For those of you who have a love for ceramics, I decided to omit a ruin and include the Papago Park Clay Pits. These pits provide a very pure reward.

Also, in the same general area, you can find the only remains of an old mansion that was built in 1910 with a pool that can be spotted off the side of the road in a thicket of cacti.

### SPECIAL NOTES:

While up by the pool, you will notice a square area that is hemmed in by a number of palm trees, and off to the right another flat area that should be explored with a metal detector.

Once, we found an old cigarette box from 1944 in that vicinity.

(Just before this book went to press, the author noticed that the pool had been filled in.)

PHOENIX

VANBUREN ST

WASHINGTON

N

ANY CAR

C CLAY PITS

R RESERVOIR

P POTTERY

O OLD 1910 POOL

M MANSION (site)

R

C

P

SRP

PARK

SMALL CANAL

SRP

RIVER BOTTOM

M

RIVER BOTTOM

O

MOEUR PARK

CURRY ROAD → SCOTTSDALE

ANY TIME

TEMPE BRIDGE

SALT RIVER

SALT RIVER

TEMPE

# 32.  *Petroglyph Canyon*

You will find the name "Pfunder" once again when you tramp around this area. Yet, this is not the main attraction.

Instead, your interests might direct you to a large group of rocks that were scribbled upon by the prehistoric Hohokam Indians.

Why did they leave their mark? Archaeologists cannot answer this question. They do not seem to believe the Pimas and Tohono O'odham tribes (Papagos) know anything about their ancestors.

However, if you want an answer, check out the ceremonial grotto by traveling this wash westwardly to its end.

**SPECIAL NOTES:**

I often wonder why some people think they know more about Indians than the Indians know about themselves.

Would you expect a Martian to know more about history on earth than you do?

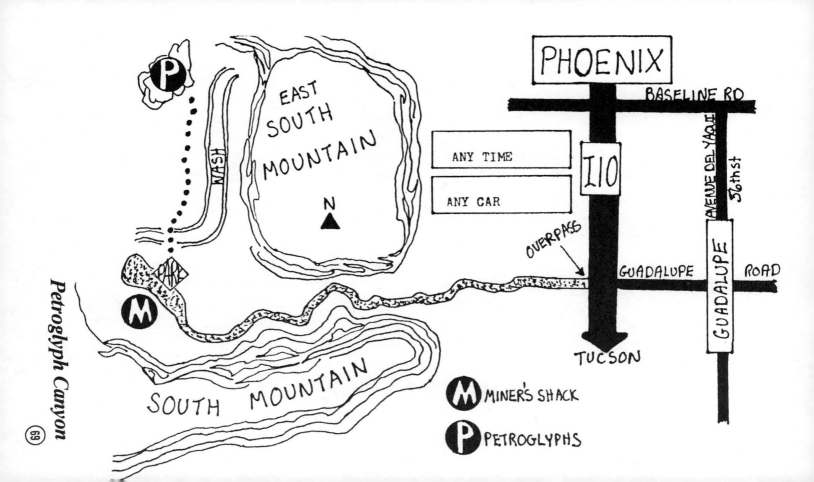

EAST SOUTH MOUNTAIN

N ▲

WASH

PHX

PHOENIX

BASELINE RD

I10

AVENUE DEL YAQUI

56th st

OVERPASS

GUADALUPE

GUADALUPE ROAD

ANY TIME

ANY CAR

TUCSON

SOUTH MOUNTAIN

Ⓜ MINER'S SHACK

Ⓟ PETROGLYPHS

# 33. *Pueblo Grande Canals*

These "canal" ruins, and the land that surrounds them, abound in a host of artifacts, arrowheads included.

Now, you know it is against the law to pick up anything but a few old bottles—things that can still be found out here by following the trails left by water runoff.

## SPECIAL NOTES:

Every winter, the Salt River Project empties their canals for repair. At this time, the canal immediately behind Pueblo Grande is also dry, and in its banks, close to the top, we have seen some beautiful quartz arrowheads that were as sharp as the day they were made.

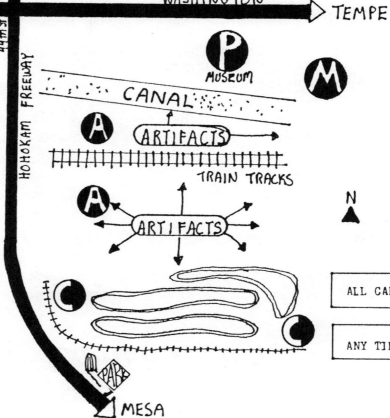

PHOENIX

WASHINGTON → TEMPE

44th St

HOHOKAM FREEWAY

**P** PUEBLO GRANDE

**M** MEAT PLANT (TORN DOWN)

**C** CANALS (PREHISTORIC)

**A** ARTIFACT SPREADS

**P** MUSEUM

**M**

CANAL

**A** ARTIFACTS

TRAIN TRACKS

**A** ARTIFACTS

**C**

**C**

PARK

MESA

N

ALL CARS

ANY TIME

# 34. Lamaide Field

This artifact spread is about all that is left of a pueblo ruin that once was equal to Pueblo Grande in size.

You will see some pottery out there, and a few arrowheads if you look hard. However, the most plentiful items seem to be a hoard of prehistoric rock tools that litter the south bank of the canal.

**SPECIAL NOTES:**

Not even these rock tools can be taken from the spot where they lie.

Nevertheless, you can look at them and study their manner of manufacture in a way that museums make impossible.

Also, the arrowheads seem to be hidden in thickets, and when you get into those shrubs, you are going to get scratched up.

Go in the early part of the spring or late fall, and wear a long-sleeved shirt, blouse or jacket.

LOWER BUCKEYE ROAD

COTTON LANE

REEMS ROAD

Ⓐ ARTIFACT SPREAD

BUCKEYE ROAD

STATE 85

PHOENIX AVONDALE

BUCKEYE

N

PLOWED FIELDS

BRIDGE

1¾ MILE

1¼ MILE

BULLARD AVENUE

Ⓐ PARK

BUCKEYE CANAL

BUCKEYE CANAL

HOME

TAKE A TRUCK

Ⓐ PARK

Ⓐ

DENSE SHRUBS

SPRING/FALL

SALT RIVER

ESTRELLA MOUNTAIN PARK

Lamaide Field
㊆

# 35. Gila Bend Ruin

Word has it that some archeologists recently worked this site.

The ground up there was once loaded with arrowheads, but now the finds are relegated to some dark basement, or the mantle piece of a pot-hunter's home.

You may still want to check it out, for it seems that some reconstruction work was done.

**SPECIAL NOTES:**

There are some items that are a must for recording your findings.
Take a camera and several rolls of film when you leave the car.
Take along a chalk line (available in any hardware store), a yard stick and a tape measure.
Bring a notebook inside a hard cover binder. You'll be glad you did.

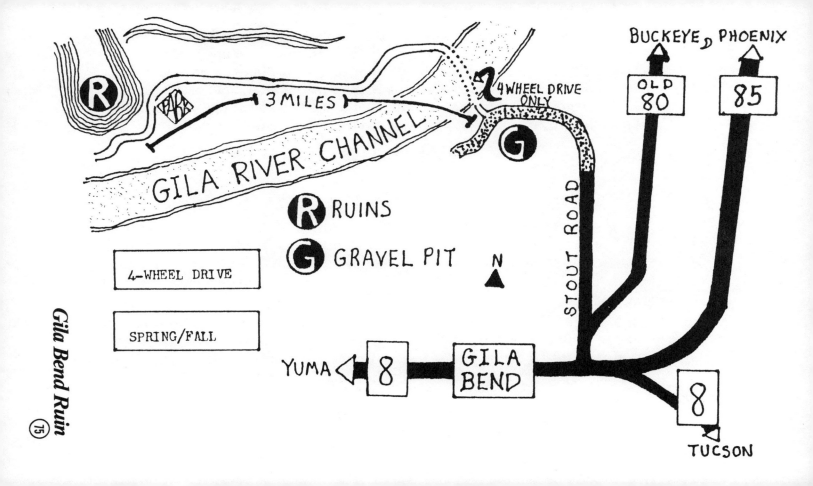

BUCKEYE PHOENIX

OLD 80

85

4 WHEEL DRIVE ONLY

3 MILES

PARK

**R**

GILA RIVER CHANNEL

**G**

**R** RUINS

**G** GRAVEL PIT

N

4-WHEEL DRIVE

SPRING/FALL

STOUT ROAD

YUMA ← 8

GILA BEND

8

TUCSON

# 36. Haufer Wash Ruin

Punkin (not pumpkin) Center and the valley of Tonto Creek comprise one of the more favored areas for Indian ruin hunting.

These are just a few of the ruins that I have "found," although I was not the first. There has been a great deal of pot hunting going on up here, but, as in the case of Haufer Wash, it has been minimal enough to allow a number of arrowheads a sense of security (at least until they are plucked up by keen eyes and greedy hands).

As for pottery and other assorted artifacts, they can only be picked up by the licensed "professional."

**SPECIAL NOTES:**

There are some things that you **DO NOT** take into any ruin, unless you are willing to pay a stiff penalty that can range into the thousands.

They include: a shovel, a hand shovel, a posthole digger, a spray paint can, or anything else that is used by morons to deface and destroy man-made or natural objects.

Once more, these are things you **DO NOT** take to a ruin.

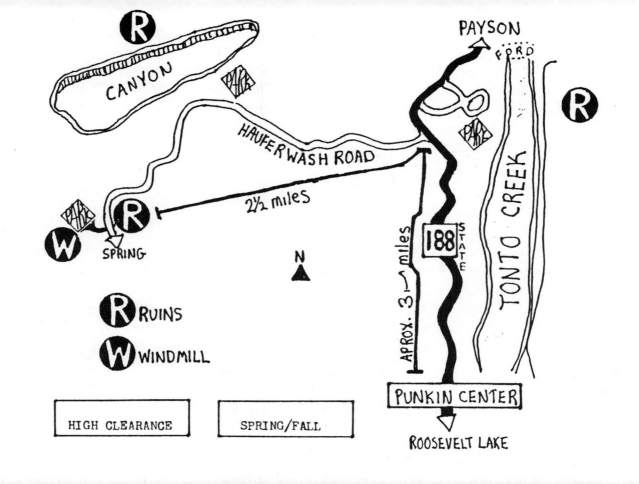

Haufer Wash Ruin
⑦

# 37. *Huens Ruin*

Huens Ruin is the one that's really far away from it all, tucked neatly out of sight in a very rugged area that is unfriendly to the sandal hiker.

True, this has felt the spade despite the seemingly "safe" location, but other than in a few spots, the ruin itself remains well intact.

Now, again I debated whether to include this ruin, but one cannot allow the acts of some vandals to rob something of unique value from the rest of us.

To lock it away so none of us can see it, that would be ridiculous. Therefore, I ask that you show a bit of respect in this ruin (and all ruins), so that future generations of explorers will have something to explore, too.

### SPECIAL NOTES:

Carry plenty of water when hiking in towards this ruin, and never, I repeat, *NEVER GO IN SUMMER!*

We almost died of dehydration, and had to drink from a cow's watering hole. You do *NOT* want to drink from one of those!

PAYSON

DANGEROUS YUCCA PATCH

FENCE

W

R

H

POWERLINES

STATE 87

OLD PUNKIN CENTER ROAD
(CLOSED)

16 MILES

N

SUNFLOWER

PHOENIX

H HUENS RUIN

R RUINED MINERS HOUSE

W WATER HOLE

HIGH CLEARANCE

EARLY SPRING

*Huens Ruin*

79

# 38. *The Mustang Ruin*

A warning about parking along this road: Do so only where you can keep an eye on your car!

The last time we climbed to this ruin, some throwback destroyed the window of my friend's car, in order to steal a couple of beers and a dead snake.

Always keep in mind that many vagrants, vandals and thieves roam these parts, too. Be careful!

As for the ruin, look into it, and take a gape at the prehistoric kiln in the middle of the village. Don't expect to find a lot of artifacts there.

**SPECIAL NOTES:**

Some of these places offer their own natural dangers, and *it is up to you to decide what you will do in these instances.*

I cannot assume, nor can my publisher assume any responsibility for your course of action.

It is up to each individual to choose. If you play it with a pinch of precaution, then you will have the opportunity to enjoy parts of Arizona that are known to a privileged few.

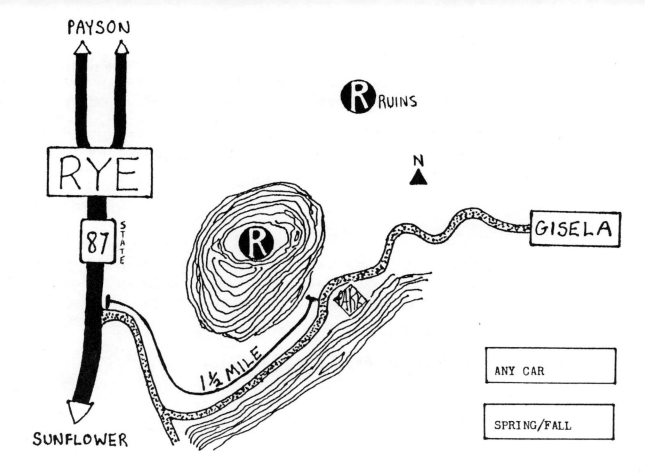

PAYSON

RYE

87 STATE

SUNFLOWER

Mustang Ruin 81

R RUINS

N

PARK

GISELA

1½ MILE

ANY CAR

SPRING/FALL

# 39. Potato Hill Ruin

Potato Hill can easily be spotted from the road which runs down the middle of Young. It is the hill that looks like a cake with a potato on top, and it is bulging with ruins that hold a lot of arrowheads.

Drive right through Young and continue toward Potato Hill.

**SPECIAL NOTES:**

Trust me when I tell you that some small town people do not like strangers. Be careful if you have long hair, if you are out hunting, hiking or biking.

While there are always many fine people in these towns, there are still some who go out of their way to make you feel unwelcome, possibly due to the remoteness of this area.

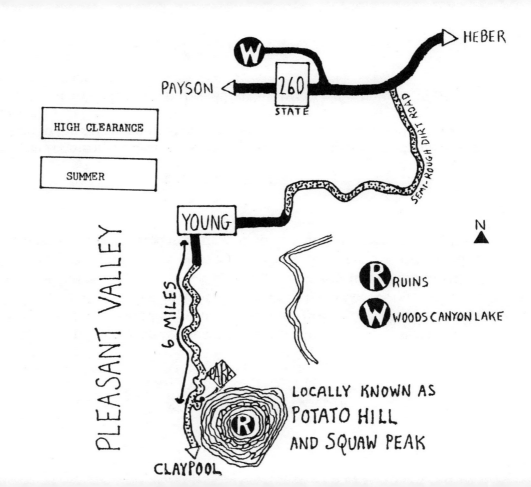

HEBER

PAYSON

260 STATE

HIGH CLEARANCE

SUMMER

YOUNG

SEMI-ROUGH DIRT ROAD

N

**R** RUINS

**W** WOODS CANYON LAKE

6 MILES

PARK

LOCALLY KNOWN AS POTATO HILL AND SQUAW PEAK

**R**

CLAYPOOL

PLEASANT VALLEY

*Potato Hill Ruin*

83

# 40. *Fossil Creek*

Fossil Creek is so-named because of a strange type of water that leaves a deposit of calcium on plant matter which gives it the appearance of fossils.

Don't fret, though. There is a vast hoard of fossils that can be located in and around the area's limestone formations.

Also, just above the springs, you will see a number of caves that still hold intact metates, bowls and similar artifacts.

These artifacts are protected by law, and it is illegal to remove anything.

**SPECIAL NOTES:**

You may come upon a situation where you find an arrowhead that is still attached to the arrow shaft. It is considered to be an arrow and cannot be removed.

Breaking it off would also be breaking the law, besides being a stupid act in the first place.

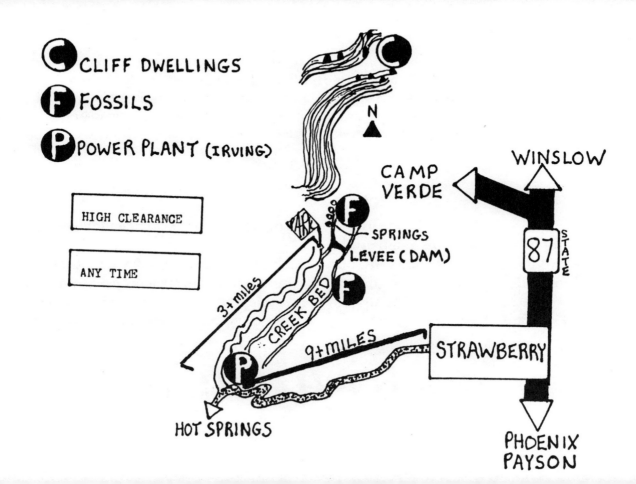

C CLIFF DWELLINGS

F FOSSILS

P POWER PLANT (IRVING)

HIGH CLEARANCE

ANY TIME

N

WINSLOW

CAMP VERDE

STATE 87

SPRINGS

LEVEE (DAM)

3+ miles

CREEK BED

9+ MILES

STRAWBERRY

HOT SPRINGS

PHOENIX PAYSON

# *41. Verde Hot Springs*

This spot along the Verde River was once the locale of a high-class resort which burnt down years ago, but this did not alter the springs in any way, shape or form.

If you happen to be one of those who is "burnt out" on the Salt, tired of camping with hundreds up on the rim, or just in need of a brief respite, bring your tent and trunks and stay here to enjoy a gift of nature that many would pay a fortune to experience.

**SPECIAL NOTES:**

There are supposed to be a number of ruins in this general area; however, we have not been so lucky as to find them.

The only information that I have is that the ruins can be found in a box canyon, one or two miles upstream from here.

HIGH CLEARANCE

WINSLOW

CAMP VERDE

16 MILES

SEE MAP #40

STRAWBERRY

87

PAYSON

OLD CAMP VERDE ROAD

N

POWER LINES

Verde Hot Springs

87

H HOTEL RUINS

S SPRINGS

P POWER STATION

VERDE RIVER

H S

P

CHILDS

SPRING/SUMMER

# 42. *Peralta Massacre Site*

You might as well forget about finding the "Lost Dutchman," for the mine was supposedly located awhile back.

Nevertheless, the Peralta Massacre site, which is at the base of a very high cliff, is the place to look for all sorts of gold.

Here, the Peralta party was ambushed by Apaches as they tried to leave the same mine with burros ladened with gold ore.

The odds are not that bad of one still finding a good chunk of the same ore—that and arrowheads, mule bones and rusted fragments of metal from colonial days.

Bring your metal detector.

## SPECIAL NOTES:

Bring plenty of water and a little common sense. This area is the favorite hangout for low-lifes that flock here from across the nation to look for gold.

In fact, we were accosted by a few religious fanatics who had found "something," but no gold. These types are more violent than the miners.

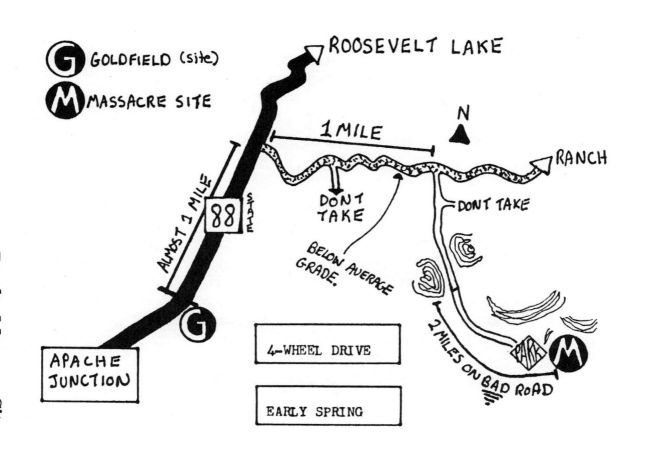

# 43. *Fish Creek Tour*

I have often spent a laborious afternoon here, sifting about for gold flakes which, more often than not, have paid for the gas expended.

You can look for gold, or pay close attention to the stream bed and loose rock along the sides for fossilized shells.

As for the mine shafts, one was being worked by a very odd person, odd in that he was friendly and showed us around the mine (which he did not own).

There's boating, fishing and booze at Apache Lake.

**SPECIAL NOTES:**

Actually, there is very little room for parking--only a few spots along the road.

My advice would be to get here early!

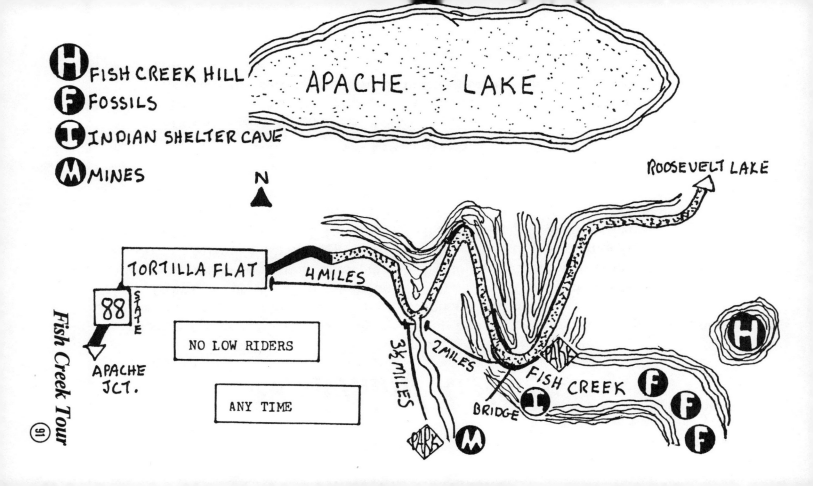

# 44. Miami Artifacts

This is a winter excursion, for only in winter can one feel comfortable in a long-sleeved shirt, a "must" when searching among the thick brush that lines both sides of the Miami Wash area.

Use a little logic and look for those flattened spots that could have given the best housing locations for the prehistoric Indians that lived here.

You should see plenty of arrowheads by doing this, but also plan on finding other artifacts that cannot be removed from the land, according to law.

## SPECIAL NOTES:

This area is also loaded with forgotten mine shafts.

The ones you can't see until you fall into them are the most hazardous. Therefore, *use some caution* when poking around, keeping an eye to the ground.

ROOSEVELT LAKE

POTTERY

ARROWHEADS

ARROWHEADS

OLD ROAD

PARK

MIAMI WASH

POTTERY

ANY CAR

WINTER ONLY

N

88 STATE

ARTIFACT LOCATIONS

CLAYPOOL

60 US

GLOBE

MIAMI

# 45. Cherry Creek

The canyons and valleys surrounding Cherry Creek are full of cliff dwellings. Undoubtedly, there are a number that still await finding.

One of the more favored ruins in this general area is that of a three-storied cliff dwelling, and is within walking distance of the Devil's Chasm.

Get here as early as you can to park, expecting to spend a greater part of your morning in following the trail that takes you to the only way into the canyon.

Everything, even the corn cobs, must be left as you find it.

**SPECIAL NOTES:**

*This road can be a killer to any vehicle other than one with high clearance.*

The worst day of my life was spent on this road in a Vega hatchback. I dropped my transmission, ran out of gas, had the radiator run dry, the car out of oil, and the electrical system partially burn out. Simply stated, make sure your car is in good shape before you attempt this trip, and bring along plenty of extra parts, water and oil. (An extra battery wouldn't hurt, either.)

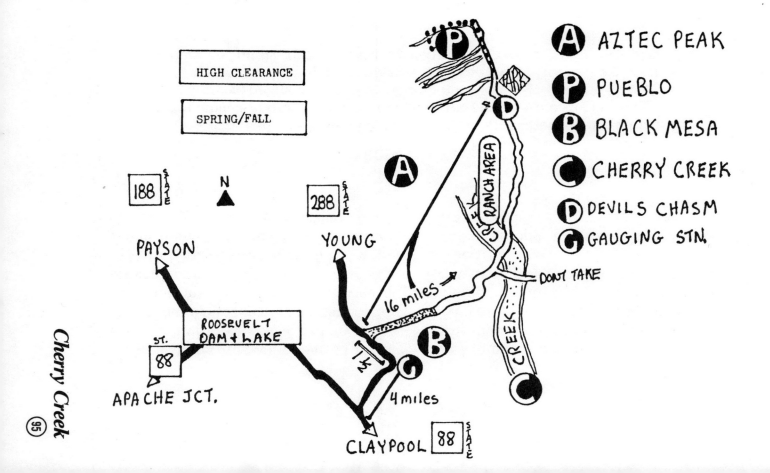

HIGH CLEARANCE

SPRING/FALL

Ⓐ AZTEC PEAK
Ⓟ PUEBLO
Ⓑ BLACK MESA
Ⓒ CHERRY CREEK
Ⓓ DEVILS CHASM
Ⓖ GAUGING STN.

STATE 188

N

STATE 288

YOUNG

PAYSON

ROOSEVELT
DAM + LAKE

ST. 88

APACHE JCT.

CREEK RANCH AREA

16 miles

DON'T TAKE

CREEK

1½

Ⓑ

Ⓖ

Ⓒ

4 miles

CLAYPOOL   STATE 88

# 46. *Reymert*

I'm a sucker for well-preserved ghost towns. This is because I've had my share of bum outings to towns that disappeared from the map without even leaving a broken bottle behind.

Most books give a vague idea of what can be found, never mentioning whether or not a trip is worth your while. That's why I jump on information concerning towns that can still be called towns.

Rest assured that there are a number of buildings awaiting you at the site of Reymert, as well as a slew of old mining artifacts.

Look around the mines for intact whiskey bottles!

## SPECIAL NOTES:

One of the saddest things about ghost towns is that they seem to attract pyromaniacs and banana cakes that think the miners were stupid enough to leave gold behind in the walls of their houses.

These people destroy ghost towns without any regard for the past or for others, and rarely get caught. If you catch one, please teach him not to play with matches.

FLORENCE

BRIDGE

SUPERIOR

60

Ⓐ

1 MILE

1¼ MILE

1¾ MILES

N

Ⓐ ARBORETUM

Ⓜ MINE SHAFTS

Ⓡ REYMERT (Ghost town)

PIPE

SPRING/FALL

HIGH CLEARANCE

Reymert

⑨⑦

# 47. Copper Hill

Copper Gulch Road will take you back into the recent past of this area, past the remains of a huge ore separator, past some old stone buildings, and into the mountains where you can find the perfect campsite for an evening.

As you wind down the road, you will spot a small white house that is built into the mountain, and upon exploration, you will find a mine entrance in the rear.

It is the perfect place to spend the night, but **stay out of this mine (and all other mines)**, as they are extremely dangerous.

Artifacts from the glory days can be found outside.

**SPECIAL NOTES:**

Not enough poems are sung about the girls of Globe. In fact, I don't know of any. They are friendly, warm and great dancers.

You ladies may want to check out the men.

COPPER GULCH ROAD

HIGH CLEARANCE

ANY TIME

N

4 MILES ON ROAD

3 MILES

**M** MINE SHAFTS

**C** COPPER HILL (ghost town)

**R** RUINED MINERS CAVE HOUSE

SHOWLOW

ST. 77

US 70

US 60

GLOBE

PHOENIX

PERIDOT

# 48. *Kinishba Ruin*

The Kinishba Ruins were excavated a long time ago, so, as you can imagine, there is little here in terms of arrowheads or other artifacts.

However, what does remain is a restored huge two-story Anasazi pueblo that can be seen without the aid of a ranger, guide or entrance fee.

Note, there is an old fence that girds the ruin, but, if this does not stop you, perhaps squatters who inhabit the pueblo will!

**SPECIAL NOTES:**

You cannot drink on the reservation. That's what a tribal policeman told us when he pulled the car over and took our beer.

**K** KINISHBA PUEBLO RUINS

SMALL WASH

PARK

SPRING/FALL

2½ MILES

N

ANY CAR

GLOBE
SHOWLOW
CARRIZO

FORT APACHE JUNCTION

1 MILE

WHITE RIVER

WHITERIVER

McNARY

STATE 73

*Kinishba Ruin*

101

# 49.  *Arsenic Cave*

Can you find your shoes in the morning?

If you are good at doing it, this is a skill that will enable you to find all of these ruins, most of which are hidden behind boulders and shrubs.

From your parking spot, a light, barely discernible trail leads to the first cliff dwelling, but from there your roving eye takes over.

One sure sign that you're near one of them is the presence of pottery shards and arrowheads at the base of the plateau.

Remember that you are still on the reservation, and since reservation laws vary from one to another, I would suggest that you **take nothing but pictures**.

**SPECIAL NOTES:**

Too many poems are sung about the girls of Arsenic Tubs, which is funny because there are no girls in Arsenic Tubs.

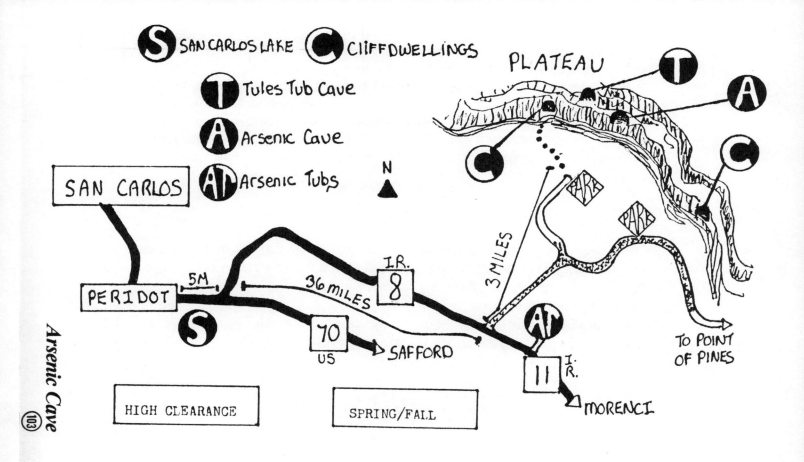

**S** SAN CARLOS LAKE   **C** Cliff Dwellings

**T** Tules Tub Cave

**A** Arsenic Cave

**AT** Arsenic Tubs

PLATEAU

SAN CARLOS

PERIDOT

5M

36 MILES

I.R. 8

70 US

SAFFORD

3 MILES

PARK

PARK

AT

11 I.R.

MORENCI

TO POINT OF PINES

HIGH CLEARANCE

SPRING/FALL

N

# 50. Eagle Creek

One day, while we were in Morenci, we learned a lot about one of the favorite local get-away spots.

The place we were directed to was a beautiful glen along Eagle Creek. Once an area inhabited by prehistoric Indians, it is now frequented by bats, but don't let them deter you from your explorations.

We also have an old cemetery that makes good pictures, a neat little spring, and just an entire day's worth of adventure in this area.

## SPECIAL NOTES:

Solid lines on my maps indicate paved roads, mottled lines mean roads that may or may not be paved, but that the road has been graded and most obstacles removed, and parallel lines mean that the road is rough, sometimes nearly invisible.

As for your mode of transportation, I make a recommendation. Small cars can travel some of these roads; some passenger cars can make others; but, you are better off with a high-clearance vehicle with four-wheel drive for most off-road purposes.

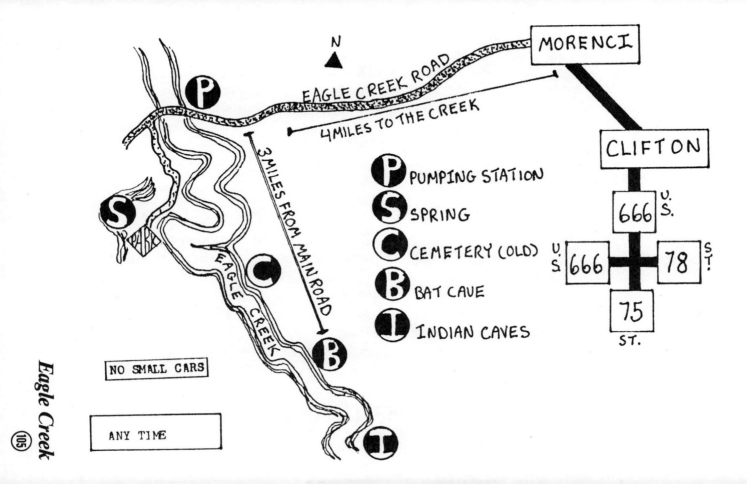

N

MORENCI

EAGLE CREEK ROAD

4 MILES TO THE CREEK

3 MILES FROM MAIN ROAD

EAGLE CREEK

**P** PUMPING STATION

**S** SPRING

**C** CEMETERY (OLD)

**B** BAT CAVE

**I** INDIAN CAVES

CLIFTON

666 U.S.

U.S. 666 | 78 ST.

75 ST.

NO SMALL CARS

ANY TIME

*Eagle Creek*

105

# 51. *Pima Butte Pottery*

Although it is illegal to gather pottery on the reservation (and elsewhere in Arizona) the next two spots are included because of the high concentration of arrowhead material.

The maps are so-named simply because of a surplus of pottery shards that literally litter the surface.

Okay. Again you are going to be faced with the temptation to stick that stray piece of pottery in your backpack, but that's something you do not want to do on the Gila River Indian Reservation.

Officials of the reservation take their heritage very seriously.

Please, don't mess it up for the rest of us by stealing pottery or other artifacts from their land.

**SPECIAL NOTES:**

The areas most likely to contain arrowheads are to be found where there is a total lack of shrubs and wild grass. This is because very few plants will grow atop the remains of an adobe ruin.

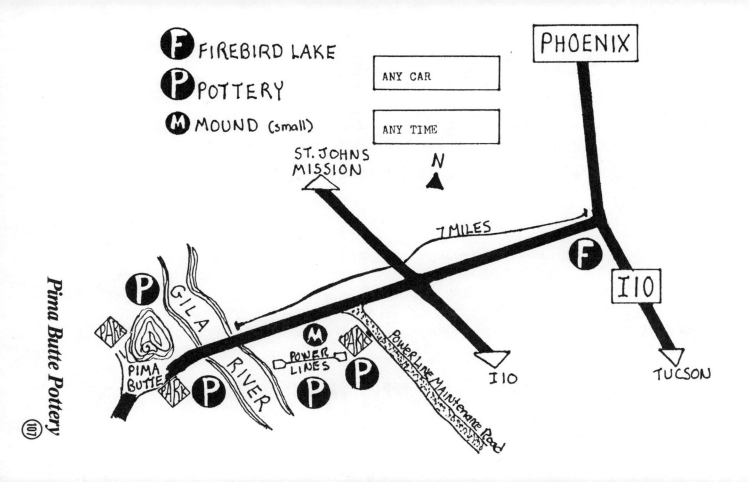

# 52. *Gila Butte Pottery*

The term "pottery" applies here, just as it did in map #51, as do the laws that protect pottery.

Now, when it comes to arrowheads, the ground around here is pretty "clean." Therefore, you must extend your search to the butte side which looks down upon the Gila River.

In and around the crevices you can locate projectile points, but this is about the only place.

**SPECIAL NOTES:**

There is an old Indian ramada standing in the middle of the field. I believe it is used for Easter services by the locals. Leave it alone!

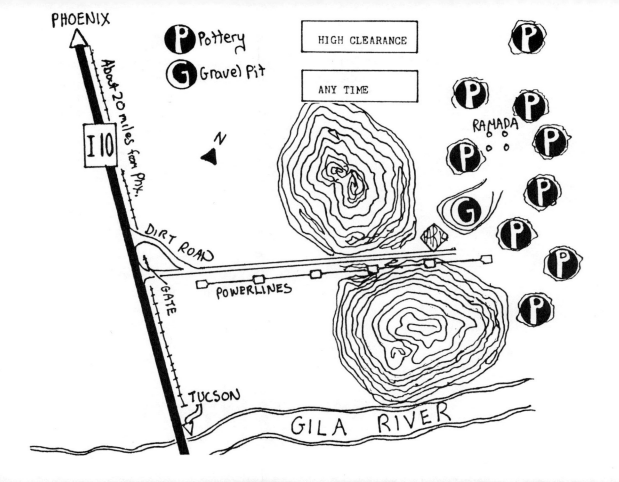

PHOENIX

About 20 miles from Phx.

I 10

P Pottery
G Gravel Pit

HIGH CLEARANCE

ANY TIME

N

DIRT ROAD

GATE

POWERLINES

RAMADA

P P P P P P P P G P P P P

BARN

TUCSON

GILA RIVER

# 53. *Marks Artifacts Spread*

This site is located right along the banks of the Gila River, and can be reached easily by almost any car.

Silt-ridden, this one spot is unsuitable for the farming that surrounds you, but seems tailor-made for the arrowhead hunter.

Look in the runoff areas to identify arrowheads and pottery shards.

Cow and horse skulls can also be found in the brush.

**SPECIAL NOTES:**

When you are in and around Indian ruins, there are a few things to watch out for.

First, the walls in these dwellings are of considerable age, some of which can give way if you lean on them, causing other things to give way such as the roof.

Also, cliff dwellings which are easily accessible to you are also just as easy to reach for wild animals, like a bobcat we went face-to-face with up around Camp Verde.

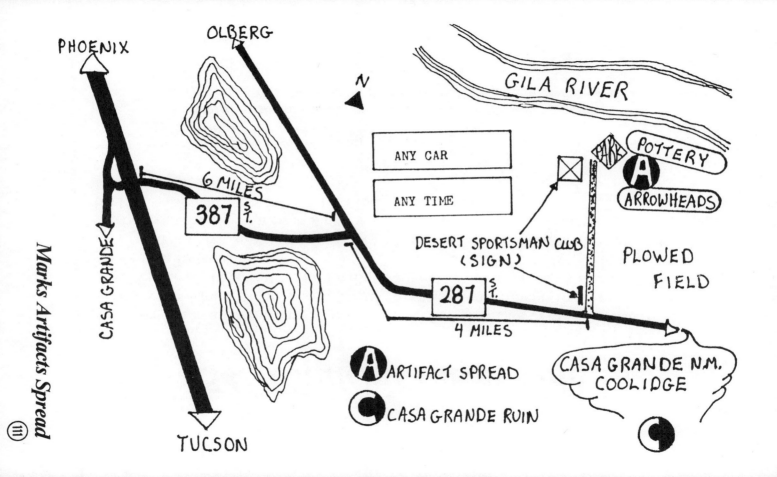

PHOENIX

OLBERG

GILA RIVER

N

CASA GRANDE

6 MILES

387 S.T.

ANY CAR

ANY TIME

PARK

POTTERY

A

ARROWHEADS

PLOWED FIELD

DESERT SPORTSMAN CLUB (SIGN)

287 S.T.

4 MILES

CASA GRANDE N.M. COOLIDGE

A ARTIFACT SPREAD

C CASA GRANDE RUIN

TUCSON

# 54. Chuichu Caves One

I swear we are never going to get off these "reservations." You know, those worthless pieces of land that we "kindly" gave to the Indians.

No coal out here, so they won't need to worry about the government asking for it back.

There are a lot of caves right across the road from Chuichu that are as good as gold to the weekend explorer.

Once used by the Hohokam, the caves now offer a real insight into the nature of Arizona's past inhabitants.

**SPECIAL NOTES:**

*Be careful in these caves*, because there are *low-lying ceilings* and *sharp, jagged sides* that could rip through leather and fake vinyl leather, too!

C CAVES

G GRAVEYARD

N ▲

PHOENIX

CASA GRANDE

GILA BEND

I8

I10

TUCSON

MILES

FLORENCE ST.

CHUICHU ROAD

ANY CAR

CHUICHU

3/4 MILE

1 MILE

G

C

SPRING/FALL

SEE MAP #55

Chuichu Caves One

113

# 55. Chuichu Caves Two

This is the place where you really want to spend the day!

The uninformed think that Apaches live in these mountains, therefore they won't come this far without the U.S. Cavalry.

Now, if you come out here, you're going to find a lot more caves than are found at Chuichu One. Also, there are some mine shafts that you want to avoid, and a nest of little Indian ruins just a short distance from the main road.

**SPECIAL NOTES:**

This area is loaded with mine shafts, and even a discarded blasting cap or two.

The mine shafts **do not want to be entered**, nor do the caps wish to be picked up. This is important to you if you want to keep your life!

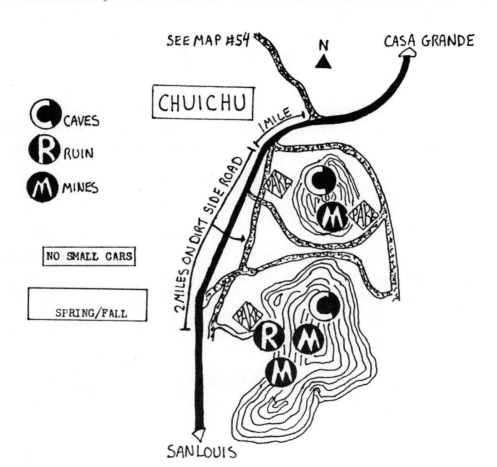

SEE MAP #54

N

CASA GRANDE

CHUICHU

1 MILE

C CAVES

R RUIN

M MINES

2 MILES ON DIRT SIDE ROAD

NO SMALL CARS

SPRING/FALL

C

M

PARK

PARK

PARK

C

R

M

M

PARK

SAN LOUIS

# 56. *Ventana Cave*

I finally managed to find this place with the aid of an archaeologist friend who, due to the nature of this work, prefers to remain obscure.

Ventana Cave is a known historical location, for it was here that evidence was found placing primitive man in this area long before the arrival of those we call Hohokam.

**SPECIAL NOTES:**

Few artifacts remain, and even these are protected by law.
This trip is meant for those who wish to see where history was made.

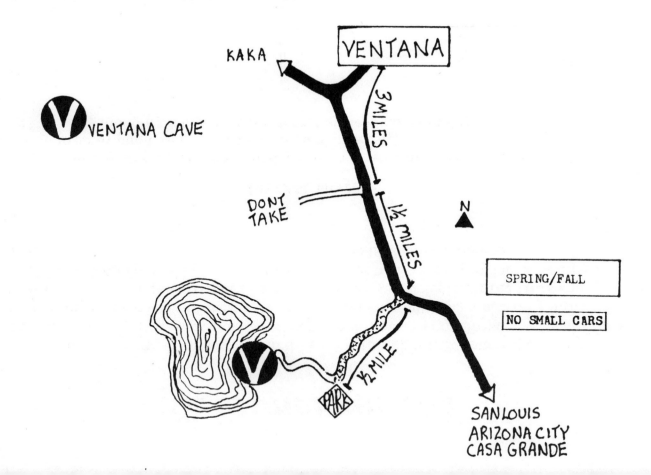

KAKA

VENTANA

V VENTANA CAVE

3 MILES

DONT TAKE

N

1½ MILES

SPRING/FALL

NO SMALL CARS

V

PARK

½ MILE

SAN LOUIS
ARIZONA CITY
CASA GRANDE

# 57. *Tumamoc Hill*

Pfunder, Pfunder, Pfunder, I found his name again. This guy should have written the book instead of me.

Anyway, if you get around Tucson, take a short jaunt to the top of Tumamoc Hill.

All along the mountainside, facing out upon Greasewood Road, you will find wall upon wall, walls which once provided a means of defense for the Hohokam.

For you, they provide a source of arrowheads to examine on the spot.

**SPECIAL NOTES:**

Psychiatrists have often puzzled over the mentality which drives people to spray paint their names on points of interest.

My thought on the subject is that they have no mentality.

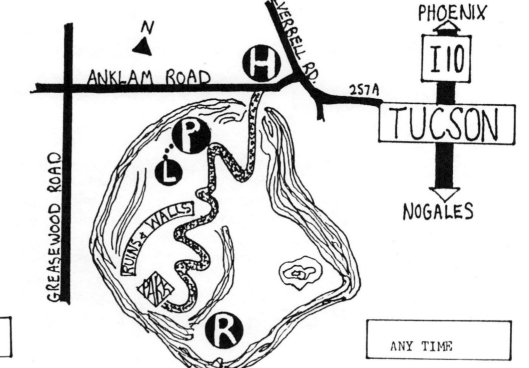

**H** HOSPITAL
**P** PETROGLYPHS
**R** RUINS
**L** UofA LAB

ANY CAR

ANY TIME

# 58. San Agustin Mission

If you are one of those camera buffs who likes to photograph the old Kino Missions, then check this one out, if you can get by without a guided tour.

Some obvious restrictions apply, as you will note, but all-in-all, I can assure you of a fun time whilst poking around the perimeter, along the Santa Cruz River, which has washed away a portion of what I think was a plaza.

The artifacts you find are also protected by law, in that they are over 100 years old. Therefore, **leave them alone!**

**SPECIAL NOTES:**

Yes, that's right, an artifact that can be dated to be more than 100 years old is protected by federal and state law.

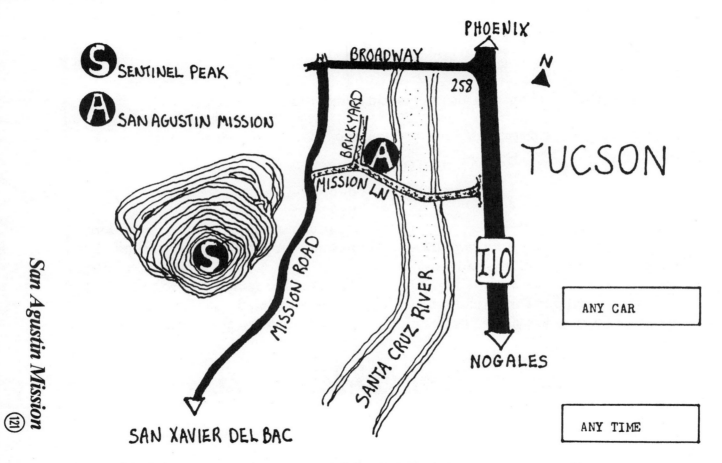

San Agustin Mission

# 59. *Peppersauce Cave*

Peppersauce Cave is known as the "party" cave of Tucson by those who are too drunk to realize that it is outside of Oracle.

Upon arriving at the pulloff, follow the beer cans to the small entrance. From there, the cave leads deep into the mountain, twisting and turning until you find that you are lost.

Go only as far as you dare, and ***do not forget your hard hat!***

## SPECIAL NOTES:

This may be a party cave, but many a drunk has cracked his skull by treating it as such.

You never want to drink in these places. You are already disoriented as it is.

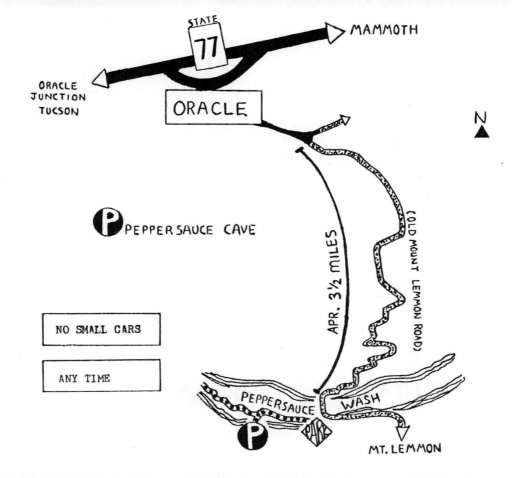

STATE
**77**

MAMMOTH

ORACLE
JUNCTION
TUCSON

ORACLE

N

PEPPERSAUCE CAVE

NO SMALL CARS

ANY TIME

APR. 3½ MILES

(OLD MOUNT LEMMON ROAD)

PEPPERSAUCE WASH

MT. LEMMON

# 60. *The Forts of Sonoita*

Let me tell you that it's well worth the cash of investing in a metal detector. When we were at the forts, we rang up a number of old buttons, bullets and the tiny tip of a sword, not to mention a few coins.

I do hope that you enjoy searching around this area, just as I will enjoy locating some more sites for my next book.

**SPECIAL NOTES:**

I cannot stress this enough: DO NOT LEND THIS BOOK TO ANYONE!

Your friends will never return it, and if they do, there will be pages missing, and beer spilled on the remaining pages.

And besides, they have been waiting for this opportunity to rip you off!

Take good care of your valued possessions and give this book to nobody.

After all, I have to eat, too!

TUCSON

**83**

RANCH

N

SONOITA **82**

2½ MILES

C

¾ MILE

B

SONOITA CREEK

NOGALES

ANY CAR

SPRING/FALL

**C** Fort Crittenden (site)

**B** Fort Buchanan (site)

*Forts of Sonoita*

125

# Index of Places
*(Numbers refer to page numbers.)*

## A-C
Adama's Cave 28, 29
Agua Fria River 53, 57, 59
Alamo Lake 47
Apache Junction 89
Apache Lake 90, 91
Arboretum 97
Arsenic Cave 102, 103
Ashfork 7
Aztec Peak 94, 95
Bartlett Lake 63, 65
Beaver Creek 22, 23, 25
Bellemont 33
Black Mesa 95
Black Mountain 11, 47
Bloody Basin 63
Bouse 43
Boynton Canyon 18, 19
Briggs 51
Camp Creek 63
Camp Verde 23, 27, 29, 34, 35
Carefree 63
Carl's Cave 28, 29
Casa Grande 113, 115
Casa Grande, N.M. 111
Castle Cleo Ruin 60, 61
Castle Creek 51
Castle Hot Springs 51
Cathedral Caves 6, 7
Cave Creek 63, 65
Cherry Creek 94, 95
Chuichu Caves 112-115
Clay Pits 66, 67
Claypool 93, 95
Clear Creek 34
Clifton 105
Clints Well 16, 17
Coolidge 111
Copper Hill 98, 99
Copperopolis 50, 51
Cornville 30, 31
Crook Trail 35
Crystal Hill 44, 45

## D-G
Date Creek 46, 47
Devil's Chasm 94, 95
Dewey 36, 37
Eagle Creek 104, 105
Estrella Mt. Park 73
Firebird Lake 107
Fish Creek 90, 91
Flagstaff 15, 17, 23, 33
Flumes 56, 57
Fort Apache 101
Fort Buchanan site 125
Fort Crittenden site 125
Fossil Creek 84, 85
Gila Bend 75
Gila Butte 108, 109

Gila River 75, 106, 107, 109, 110, 111
Gisela 81
Globe 99
Goldfield 89
Guadalupe 69

## H-L
Hancock Ranch 21
Hassayampa Lake, River 41
Haufer Wash 76, 77
Horseshoe Lake 63, 65
Horsethief Basin 41
Huens Ruin 78, 79
Humboldt Observatory 63
Ice Caves 11, 32
Indian Mesa 52, 53
Kingston Ruins 12, 13
Kinishba 100, 101
Lake Montezuma 24, 25
Lake Pleasant 51, 57, 59
Lamaide Field 72, 73
Lava River Cave 32, 33
Little Colorado River 8, 9
Lomaki Ruin 8, 9
Lost Dutchman Mine 88
Loy Butte 20, 21
Lynx Creek 38, 39

## M-O
Marks 110, 111
McGuireville 25
Miami 92, 93
Miami Wash 92, 93
Moeur Park 67
Monte Cristo Mine 41
Montezuma Lake 24, 25
Montezuma's Castle 26, 27, 29
Montezuma's Well 23
Morenci 105
Mormon Lake 16, 17
Morristown 51
Mount St. Claire 64, 65
Munds Park 17
Mustang Ruin 80, 81
New River 53, 55
Nipper Falls 62
Nipper Ruin 58, 59
Oak Creek 19, 30, 31
Oracle 122, 123
Other Castle 26, 27

## P-R
Papago Park 66, 67
Partridge Creek 7
Payson 81, 83, 85, 87
Peppersauce 122, 123
Peralta Massacre site 88, 89
Peridot 103
Petroglyph Canyon 68, 69
Pfunder 54, 55

Phoenix 59, 61, 63, 67, 69, 71, 107, 109
Pima Butte 106, 107
Planet Ranch 43
Pleasant Valley 83
Potato Hill 82, 83
Prescott 36, 37, 39, 41
Prescott Valley 39
Pueblo Grande 70, 71
Punkin Center 76, 77, 79
Quartz Mountain 46, 47
Quartzsite 45
Red Canyon Ranch 21
Reymert 96, 97
Rye 81

## S
Sacred Mountain 22, 23
Salt River 67, 73
San Agustin Mission 120, 121
San Carlos 103
San Francisco Wash 13
San Louis 115, 117
Sedona 19, 21
Senator 40, 41
Sentinel Peak 121
Seven Springs 62, 63
Sonoita 124, 125
South Mountain 69
Strawberry 34, 35, 85, 87
Strawberry Crater 10, 11
Sugarloaf Mountain 30, 31
Sun City 57, 59
Sunflower 79
Sunset Crater 11, 32
Superior 97
Swansea 42, 43
Sycamore Canyon 35

## T-Z
Tonto Creek 76, 77
Tortilla Flat 91
Tucson 119, 121
Tules Tub Cave 103
Tumamoc Hill 118, 119
Ventana Cave 116, 117
Venzia 40, 41
Verde Hot Springs 86, 87
Verde River 27, 29, 30, 31, 34, 35, 86, 87
Vicksburg 45
Vultee Arch 19
Vulture Mine 48, 49
Walnut Canyon N.M. 14, 15
White River 101
Wickenburg 46, 47, 49
Wild Bill Hill 33
Wingfield 34, 35
Winona 13
Wupatki N.M. 8, 9
Young 82, 83

Order from your book dealer or direct from publisher.

# ▪▪▪▪▪▪▪▪▪▪▪▪▪ *ORDER BLANK* ▪▪▪▪▪

*Explore ARIZONA!*
by Rick Harris

# Golden West Publishers

4113 N. Longview Ave.,
Phoenix, AZ 85014

Please ship the following books:

_____ Arizona Adventure ($5.00)

_____ Arizona Cook Book ($3.50)

_____ Arizona Museums ($5.00)

_____ Arizona—Off the Beaten Path ($4.50)

_____ Arizona Outdoor Guide ($5.00)

_____ California Favorites Cook Book ($3.50)

_____ Chili-Lovers' Cook Book ($3.50)

_____ Citrus Recipes ($3.50)

_____ Cowboy Slang ($5.00)

_____ Explore Arizona ($5.00)

_____ Fools' Gold (Lost Dutchman Mine) ($5.00)

_____ Ghost Towns in Arizona ($4.50)

_____ Greater Phoenix Street Maps Book ($4.00)

_____ How to Succeed in Selling Real Estate ($3.50)

_____ In Old Arizona ($5.00)

_____ Mexican Cook Book ($5.00)

I enclose $ _____ (including $1 per order postage, handling).

Name _____

Address _____

City _____ State \_\_\_\_\_ Zip_____

**This order blank may be photo copied**

# Books from Golden West Publishers

Read of the daring deeds and exploits of Wyatt Earp, Buckey O'Neill, the Rough Riders, Arizona Rangers, cowboys, Power brothers shootout, notorious Tom Horn, Pleasant Valley wars, "first" American revolution—action-packed true tales of early Arizona! *Arizona Adventure (by Marshall Trimble), 160 pages . . . $5.00.*

The lost hopes, the lost lives—the lost gold! Facts, myths and legends of the Lost Dutchman Gold Mine and the Superstition Mountains. Told by a geologist who was there! *Fools' Gold (by Robert Sikorsky), 144 pages . . . $5.00.*

Take the back roads to and thru Arizona's natural wonders—Canyon de Chelly, Wonderland of Rocks, Monument Valley, Rainbow Bridge, Four Peaks, Swift Trail, Alamo Lake, Virgin River Gorge, Palm Canyon, Red Rock Country! *Arizona—off the beaten path! (by Thelma Heatwole), 144 pages . . . $4.50.*

Plants, animals, rocks, minerals, geologic history, natural environments, landforms, resources, national forests and outdoor survival—with maps, photographs, drawings, charts, index. *Arizona Outdoor Guide (by Ernest E. Snyder), 126 pages . . . $5.00*

Visit the silver cities of Arizona's golden past with this prize-winning reporter-photographer. Come along to the towns whose heydays were once wild and wicked! See crumbling adobe walls, old mines, cemeteries, cabins and castles. *Ghost Towns and Historical Haunts in Arizona (by Thelma Heatwole), 144 pages . . . $4.50.*

Colorful, down-to-earth expressions of the American cowboy—2,000 of them—are captured by **"Frosty" Potter** and illustrated by **Ron Scofield**. Includes horse and cattle terms, rodeo talk, barb wire history, cattle brands. *Cowboy Slang, 128 pages . . . $5.00.*